Worth

Divine Beginnings, Happy Endings

Worth

Divine Beginnings, Happy Endings

WENDY ELLISON

Covenant Communications, Inc.

Cover Image: *Dawning Light* © Annie Henrie Nader. For more information, please visit www.anniehenrie.com

Cover design copyright © 2018 by Covenant Communications, Inc.

Published by Covenant Communications, Inc.
American Fork, Utah

Printed in the United States of America
First Printing: March 2018

24 23 22 21 20 19 18   10 9 8 7 6 5 4 3 2 1

ISBN: 978-1-52440-503-8

For Mom and Dad

Contents

Introduction

IN A LIFE BEFORE THIS and in a place we can't remember, we lived with God. He is our loving Father and our Heavenly King. We are members of His royal family. While we cannot recollect what it was like there or even that we were there, we know from revelation some important truths about who we are and our relationship with Him. In Jeremiah we read, "Before I formed thee in the belly I knew thee" (Jer. 1:5). In Isaiah we find, "I have called thee by thy name; thou art mine" (Isa. 43:1). Job said, "The Spirit of God hath made me, and the breath of the Almighty hath given me life" (Job 33:4). And from a passage in the Doctrine and Covenants, we discover that Jesus was in the beginning with the Father and that we were as well (see D&C 93:21).

Church leaders in our day have also shared their witnesses. Elder Neal A. Maxwell said, "I testify to you that God has known you individually . . . for a long, long time (see D&C 93:23). He has loved you for a long, long time. He not only knows the names of all the stars (see Ps. 147:4; Isa. 40:26); He knows your names and all your heartaches and your joys!"[1]

President Dieter F. Uchtdorf said, "You are known and remembered by the most majestic, powerful, and glorious Being in the universe! You are loved by the King of infinite space and everlasting time!"[2]

And Sister Rosemary M. Wixom testified, "Our divine nature comes from God. It was established in an existence that preceded our birth and will continue on into eternity."[3]

It's both humbling and reassuring that God, who has power to create galaxies and control the elements, has a personal interest in our lives and that

---

1 Neal A. Maxwell, "Remember How Merciful the Lord Hath Been," *Ensign*, May 2004, 46.
2 Dieter F. Uchtdorf, "Forget Me Not," *Ensign*, Nov. 2011, 123.
3 Rosemary M. Wixom, "Discovering the Divinity Within," *Ensign*, Nov. 2015, 6.

the title of Father is the one He esteems most. He knows our names and our needs, and He has from the beginning. Our lives didn't begin here, and they won't end here. We are eternal beings. Our journey here is just a small segment of our eternal life.

We don't remember our association with Heavenly Father, but just because a veil was drawn when we left our heavenly home doesn't mean we left everything behind. We came to this earth with our eternal identity intact. Through the vast expanse of space and time, nothing can change the truth that we are His, beloved daughters of the King of Heaven.

In medieval times, mortal kings built castles. Though we often see them depicted as fancy living quarters for fairy-tale princesses, the stone exteriors, tall towers, drawbridges, and vast moats also served another purpose. They protected and defended the interests and lives of the royals who resided there. The threat of invasion and overthrow at the hands of enemies was real, as was the possibility of uprising from a king's own subjects. The sturdy structures were fortresses where offensives were launched and kingdoms were defended in the event of an attack.

The battles we wage daily are different than the physical combat waged on an ancient battlefield. They don't involve knights in shining armor, shields, swords, clubs, or catapults, but the enemy is just as real. The adversary would like to disrupt our spiritual and physical safety and security. He works actively to define and demean our roles as women of God. One of the tools he uses is attacks on our self-worth. If he can get us to question ourselves, to wonder if we will ever measure up, to the point of giving up or forgetting about our eternal relationship with our heavenly parents and about our purpose on this earth, he can go a long way in preventing us from reaching our true destiny and divine potential.

In His great wisdom and love, our Heavenly Father constructed a plan with the necessary direction to fortify and protect our lives, just as those castles protected their inhabitants. In like manner, one of our greatest responsibilities as women is to fortify ourselves, our homes, and our families, to strengthen and keep them safe in a world of ever-increasing opposition and eroding values. Understanding our eternal worth and following our Father's plan will build us so we will have the power and resolve to avoid the stumbling blocks and pitfalls the adversary puts in our paths. Our Father's plan is our best chance of finding happiness and safety in this life. Ultimately, it enables us to find our way back to Him.

As a loving parent, our Heavenly Father hopes for us, helps us, and is everlastingly aware of our potential, even when we're not. He has promised us blessings unmeasured—more than any accolade or reward we could ever hope to attain in mortality. He wants us to be part of His kingdom here, and He wants us to be part of His heavenly kingdom when life on earth is over. We are more effective in the work He has for us to do when we are filled with confidence and a deep sense of our eternal purpose and worth to carry us through. Knowing who we are and what we are here to do makes all the difference. In the chapters of this book, we will talk a little about both.

Chapter One
The Princess in Aisle Nine

*You were sent away from a royal court without memory of who you are or what your
final role and responsibility will be. Each of you are of a royal birth and heritage.
You are a . . . daughter of heavenly parents. You are destined to become a . . . queen.*[4]
—Allan F. Packer

IF I'D KNOWN THERE WAS going to be a princess in the fabric store that morning,
I would have dressed for the occasion. I don't have a single formal ball gown
lying about the house, but I'm certain I had something more appropriate for a
brush with royalty than worn-out jeans and an old T-shirt. Not every shopper
knew about the princess in the store that day. I was only aware because of a
conversation I overheard in the aisle next to me. It's surprising I paid attention.
I was preoccupied with finding just the right embellishment for an overdue
project when I heard the brief exchange.

"I'm a princess," a tiny voice said.

There was a very short pause.

"I know you are," a fellow shopper whispered, a hint of enchantment in
her voice. "I could tell right away."

I guessed from the sound of her voice that the princess wasn't older than
three or four. At first I wanted to sneak around the corner and take a peek,
but I didn't want to intrude, and I didn't really need to look. Having raised
a few princesses of my own, I had a pretty good idea of how she might have
been dressed—feather boa, plastic beads, and a sparkling crown. (I've also
seen numerous princesses clomping in their glittery heels at shopping malls,
grocery stores, and even a baseball game or two.)

Unlike the little one who made the announcement, the respondent was a
grown woman, maybe my age, maybe older. I loved what she said, and I wondered
if I would have thought to say the same, especially so quickly.

4 Allan F. Packer, "Finding Your Way" (Brigham Young University devotional, Jan. 12, 2016);
speeches.byu.edu.

It was a short conversation—a moment, and then it was over—but it was magical nonetheless. It has stayed with me through the years as I've wondered at its implications. Why do little girls believe they are princesses? (Almost all of them do.) And how is it that as we leave those fairy-tale days behind, time steals some of the pixie dust and magic spells that used to be part of our dreams? I suppose it has something to do with a real life that is often far less glamorous than enchanted evenings, glass slippers, and sequined gowns. (And in my humble opinion, it could very well be directly tied to toilet cleaning and ironing, in particular.)

Some of my favorite movie lines come from a film adaptation of the book by Frances Hodgson Burnett entitled, *A Little Princess*. In the movie, Sara Crewe and her father have just arrived at Miss Minchin's boarding school, where Sara will reside while Mr. Crewe is away at war. Her privileged childhood is apparent as she is granted all the finest accommodations the school has to offer.

After a short time there, at her birthday party no less, Sara learns that her beloved father is missing in action and presumed dead. Up to this very moment, no expense has been spared for Sara. But with her father's assets frozen and financial support gone, Miss Minchin, the nasty headmistress, immediately forces her into servitude to pay back the debt. The little princess is removed of all of her possessions and banished to the rat-infested attic where she stays when she isn't performing menial tasks or serving her former peers.

One evening, Miss Minchin discovers some of Sara's school friends in her attic room, listening with rapt attention to her captivating stories—they all loved her whimsical tales when she was a student like them. The headmistress is instantly enraged when she finds the other girls there and dismisses them at once to deal with them later. Alone with Sara, Miss Minchin is amazed that the young girl doesn't seem to understand her new place in life. In an angry response to Sara's apparent refusal to accept her situation, Miss Minchin exclaims, "Don't tell me you still fancy yourself a princess. Look around you. Or better yet, look in the mirror."[5]

Sara's brave and telling reply follows: "I am a princess. All girls are. Even if they live in tiny old attics, even if they dress in rags, even if they aren't pretty or smart or young, they're still princesses, all of us. Didn't your father ever tell you that?"[6]

Silenced by Sara's boldness, Miss Minchin slinks away. In that moment, not only do we learn something about Miss Minchin but we discover something about Sara as well. She hasn't cowered in a corner or let her circumstances define how she feels about herself, because she knows who she is.

We know too. We *are* of royal birth, daughters of a Heavenly King. Our <u>Father</u> *has* told us that. That knowledge instills a quiet confidence and carries us

5 *A Little Princess*, directed by Alfonso Cuarón (Warner Bros. 1995).
6 Ibid.

forward in what we are doing, where we are going, and what we can become. Each of us has the potential to be queens in our Father's eternal realm. President Boyd K. Packer said it this way: "Spiritually you are of noble birth, the offspring of the King of Heaven. Fix that truth in your mind and hold to it. However many generations in your mortal ancestry, no matter what race or people you represent, the pedigree of your spirit can be written on a single line. You are a child of God!"[7]

Because of this divine definition, even when we get discouraged or doubt ourselves, nothing can change our worth—not what we do, what we look like, how old we grow, or anything else for that matter. In spite of this truth, even as we understand that self-esteem is a variable assessment of how we feel about ourselves, sometimes it gets all tied up with our real worth. It's vital to recognize the difference in a world that often sends a conflicting message. We must never forget that our worth is constant, unchanging, and inherent as daughters of God.

President James E. Faust shared this thought: "Who you *think* you are and who you *really* are can be two different versions of yourself. From an eternal perspective, these two versions need to come together. God knows you and what you can become because He has known you from the beginning when you were His spirit . . . daughters."[8]

From generation to generation, our brothers and sisters across the globe have asked the age-old questions, "Who am I?" "Why am I here?" "Where am I going?" Fortunately for us, each of those questions has been answered scripturally and by ancient and modern prophets and other leaders who want to help us understand. The answers have remained the same across time. So who are we? Sister Sheri Dew said, "Noble and great. Courageous and determined. Faithful and fearless. That is who you are, and that is who you have always been. Understanding that truth can change your life, because this knowledge carries a confidence that cannot be duplicated any other way."[9]

Our Heavenly Father has work for us to do, promises to keep, and a divine personal mission only we can fulfill. It is the opportunity of a lifetime and our noble responsibility to answer His call, learn what He wants us to do, and follow His counsel. As we do, we will have Him near us always. Ultimately, our grandest desire and the very purpose of our existence is to have a place at His side when we return home after our work here is completed.

In a premortal realm, we were with our Heavenly Father, learning and progressing, before we left His presence. He sent us to earth as infants, helpless

7 Boyd K. Packer, "The Message: A Few Simple Lessons," *New Era*, Aug. 2002, 7.

8 James E. Faust, "Who Do You Think You Are?" *Ensign*, Mar. 2001, 6.

9 Sheri L. Dew, "Knowing Who You Are—and Who You Have Always Been" (Brigham Young University Women's Conference, May 4, 2001); womensconference.byu.edu.

and innocent, forgetting all we knew, to begin our learning and proving process here. A passage of scripture confirms, "Even before they were born, they, with many others, received their first lessons in the world of spirits and were prepared to come forth in the due time of the Lord to labor in his vineyard for the salvation of the souls of men" (D&C 138:56).

In the familiar and oft-quoted verse, William Wordsworth poetically reflects on what we too know about our eternal identity:

> Our birth is but a sleep and a forgetting:
> The soul that rises with us, our life's Star,
> Hath elsewhere its setting,
> And cometh from afar:
> Not in entire forgetfulness,
> And not in utter nakedness,
> But trailing clouds of glory, do we come
> From God, who is our home[10]

When considering a sweet and innocent infant so recently in the presence of our Heavenly Father, it isn't hard to picture bits of heaven coming with them at birth, a spark of the divine. You may not have noticed it recently, but if you look very carefully, perhaps with spiritual eyes, that light and glorious promise are still there—no matter how old you grow. Due to the nature of our birth and from whence we came, heavenly light and unending potential stay with us throughout our lives and beyond, even if we can't sense or see them.

What is one of the first things we do after we learn the vital statistics of a brand-new baby? We usually try to identify who he or she resembles most. Are those Mom's eyes? Is that Dad's nose? While recognizable physical traits are often easy to detect, as children grow, mannerisms and qualities also start to come through loud and clear. This thought was recently confirmed to me by something my husband and I noticed simultaneously on a shopping trip to a local home decor store. We were fortunate enough to be assisted by a wonderful young man in our ward. I didn't know he worked there, but it was our pleasure to visit with him for a few minutes while he helped us. What I realized then that I hadn't noticed before was that he is absolutely the younger version of his dad. It isn't as much the physical likeness, though there is some of that. I realized that if I had closed my eyes and listened to the way he spoke—the inflections in his voice—I would have guessed it was his father,

10 William Wordsworth, *Select Poems of William Wordsworth,* edited by M. F. Libby, B. A. (Toronto: The Copp, Clark Company, Limited, 1892), 99.

instead of him, talking to me. My husband and I spoke about it as we left the store and were both astonished we had missed it until that moment, since the similarities are so remarkable. I wasn't always very good at identifying family resemblances. Now that I am older, I look for them all the time because I find it fascinating. Savannah and Michael and Olivia and Sam—you get the picture—all miniature versions of one parent or the other or a delightful combination of the two.

Just as we are born with qualities and characteristics from our earthly parents, we've also inherited traits—a portion of divinity—from our heavenly parents so that we may, in time, become like Them. We may not always recognize all those qualities immediately, but as mortals we possess them in various stages of development. It is our ultimate hope to develop them in the measure our heavenly parents possess them. That is the quest of a lifetime. In the meantime, we are invited to discover and expand these qualities for our own enrichment as well as for the benefit of others.

Some of the attributes of godliness were eloquently outlined long ago by the Savior's chief Apostle, Peter, and are to be sought after and incorporated into our lives. He wrote, "Be partakers of the divine nature . . . giving all diligence, add to your faith virtue; and to virtue knowledge; and to knowledge temperance; and to temperance patience; and to patience godliness; and to godliness brotherly kindness; and to brotherly kindness charity" (2 Pet. 1:4–7).

Though we are full of promise and infinite potential, we as women also have the tendency to be especially hard on ourselves. Why? There are many and varied reasons. For starters, maybe we are occasionally guilty of letting insignificant standards of worth influence the real definition, even though we don't intend to. But doing so is detrimental to our physical and spiritual well-being and can cause us to question who we are or to compare ourselves to others in an unhealthy way. Most of us are expert at identifying and judging harshly our sundry faults and flaws, even when we can ignore or accept the weaknesses of others. We have a hard time forgiving ourselves. It's possible you've noticed that pesky trait in yourself or others. We often feel pressure to do everything well, to be everything. We compare ourselves to others, to their accomplishments and talents. We are frequently guilty of holding up our worst in comparison to another's very best and then wondering why we feel like we can't measure up.

Have you ever looked at yourself in one of those silly funhouse mirrors at an amusement park? When I was a little girl, my friends and I laughed out loud at the distorted images they reflected back at us. But sometimes, the way we see ourselves is just as out of proportion as the image in those mirrors because we just might base how we feel about our reflection on criteria that isn't very important.

As Sister Rosemary M. Wixom said, "Looking out through a window, not just into a mirror, allows us to see ourselves as His."[11]

I haven't stepped inside a funhouse since I was a girl. As I've grown older, I don't generally find humor in any mirror, distorted or otherwise. Unfortunately for me, there is a glass door right outside my office at work that reminds me very much of those misleading mirrors. It makes my hips look big. I've made a habit of avoiding it as much as I can by hugging the wall as I walk that way or by going down another hall and entering my office from the other direction. A female coworker and I were complaining about it one day and wondering out loud why the glass door had to be *there*, where we see it all the time. A male colleague overheard our conversation. (Note: He hadn't even considered how his hips or anything else looked in that glass.) He took a sticky note and wrote by hand, *Like U 4 U* and stuck it to the door. He is absolutely right! But that is easier said than done. Unless I'm completely out of touch with how a woman's mind works, I believe we don't generally look at our reflections and contemplate how lovely our spirits are, even though we should. Sometimes it's hard to get to the inside because we tend to find fault with what is on the outside first.

And as if we aren't hard enough on ourselves, there's the constant bombardment of airbrushed images in movies and magazines that depict physical flawlessness. It's easy to feel inadequate if our dress size, shoe size, nose size—the list goes on and on—isn't currently deemed ideal by society today. These unfair estimations often have an unreasonable amount to do with how we feel about ourselves. But basing our worth on unattainable standards only leads us on a never-ending quest for self-esteem, because the fictional ideal simply doesn't exist.

What if we started seeing ourselves and others through our Heavenly Father's eyes? What if we bravely decided today to base the way we feel about ourselves on our eternal worth as daughters of God? What if we made a pact to forget about comparisons and evaluate ourselves on what really matters? What if we gave ourselves permission to love *us* unconditionally?

I know it's not as easy as it sounds, and it would be naïve to suggest that we won't struggle at times to see ourselves as we really are. But who we are as daughters of God is the only reliable assessment of our worth. We shouldn't base it on anything except the eternal measures our loving Father has established.

Perhaps we could take a cue from a friend's four-year-old daughter, who attended a temple open house. When one of the volunteers welcomed her there and introduced herself, the little girl replied, "Hello, I'm Princess Kathryn." And

11 Rosemary M. Wixom, "Discovering the Divinity Within," *Ensign*, Nov. 2015, 6.

she didn't just say it; she believes it. I hope she always will. Sara Crewe, Kathryn, and the little girl in the fabric store are right: they are princesses. That doesn't change just because we're grown. But it's not really about a title, coronation, or designation. There is much more in store for us! We are all daughters of the King of Heaven—striving to be humble, grateful, generous women—in line to receive all He has. Because of our royal heritage and because we are heirs of His blessings, the possibilities for us are endless. We have potential to become queens; recipients of thrones, principalities, and powers (see D&C 132:19); to be crowned with glory (see 1 Pet. 5:4); and to be clothed forever in the robes of righteousness (see Isa. 61:10).

Chapter Two
The Price He Paid

If we could truly understand the Atonement of the Lord Jesus Christ, we would realize how precious is one son or daughter of God.[12] —M. Russell Ballard

NOT ONLY IS OUR WORTH evident in our noble birthright but it is also inseparably tied to the Savior's Atonement in our behalf. What Jesus Christ did for all mankind, He also did for each of us individually. And He did it because we are worth it.

When she was young, our oldest daughter, Whitney, hoped there was a treasure or at least a valuable trinket tucked away in some forgotten corner of our home. She was first intrigued by the possibility because of a PBS television show she watched called *Antiques Roadshow*. Our family occasionally watched with her as hopeful collectors brought their prized treasures for professional appraisal. Experts evaluated the collectibles based on a number of criteria, including condition, age, and market demand.

During an episode we watched together, a woman presented a chair she had previously purchased at an estate sale. To my untrained eye, it looked exactly like an old chair—okay, a really old chair. On the other hand, the experienced appraiser saw its value immediately and was enthusiastic as he shared what he knew about the antique. He and the owner laughed together as she described the ridicule she'd endured from her family when she first brought the prehistoric piece of furniture home. As it turned out, the owner of the chair got the last laugh. The expert confirmed what the astute shopper had suspected all along. The chair was worth a fortune—hundreds of thousands of dollars—far more than the nominal price she'd paid for it. Afterward we learned that the chair sold for much more than even the appraised value.

---

12 M. Russell Ballard, "The Atonement and the Value of One Soul," *Ensign*, May 2004, 88.

Since the only remarkable find I've ever known was a five-dollar grill I stumbled on at an early bird sale, I wondered how any chair could be worth that kind of money, even an ancient one. My husband offered a simple explanation that stuck with me because of its deeper meaning. In short, he said that value was based on market demand, and market demand was driven by whatever price prospective buyers were willing to pay. Consider this. If the value of an old chair is determined by what someone will pay for it, imagine our worth based on the ultimate price our Savior paid for us. The scriptures remind us that we were "bought with a price" (1 Cor. 6:20). Though the price was steep and staggering indeed, He generously offered His all without the slightest thought of repayment or reward.

We know that in the councils of heaven our Father asked for a volunteer to carry out His plan. Before we were ever born, Jesus Christ stepped forward, motivated by love alone and not by the desire for personal gain as another selfishly sought. We discover remarkable meaning to our lives as we recognize that our Savior suffered all He did because He loves us more than we can comprehend. He said, "Greater love hath no man than this, that a man lay down his life for his friends" (John 15:13). We *are* His friends. He endured the anguish of the garden; the cruel betrayal of one friend and the denial three times of another; the scourging and mocking; and finally, the Crucifixion, for us. Clearly, He wouldn't have sacrificed all He did to save us if we weren't worth saving.

I've committed a favorite poem to memory because of its spectacular message. It would be well-placed on a refrigerator, bathroom mirror, or tucked away in some scriptures. I recite it to myself whenever I am lacking confidence and need a reminder that my worth is infinitely tied to our Elder Brother's act of Atonement.

> I am worth the coming down,
> the silence
> in return for mockery.
> I am worth the thorns,
> the bleeding back,
> the wincing, weakening steps to Calvary.
> He suffered these and thought of me.
> He could have halted soldiers
> with a fiery eye,
> And pronounced death
> in words that rang
> from marble palace walls,

And in the garden dreamed instead of prayed.
But as the glistening crimson beads
slipped from his face,
He thought that I was worth the price he paid.
I'm blind to what
He sees in me,
Yet I know thorns
and what it is
to wince and weaken.
Gethsemane and Calvary—
He suffered so
and thought of me.[13]

Sister Camille Fronk Olson once wrote, "One of the most profound realizations of individual worth comes when we recognize Christ's suffering for us."[14] We know that in the face of unimaginable suffering, He didn't shrink but fulfilled His mission for each of us individually. Knowing this, why wouldn't we base how we feel about ourselves on His opinion rather than on some superficial assessment or on the critical way we sometimes view ourselves?

In our world, worth is often calculated on a sliding scale. The emphasis on what is esteemed in society changes frequently as different traits and trends or definitions of success go in and out of style. In addition, importance is often placed on things that don't matter very much. That type of estimation has always been unreliable. On the other hand, our Savior's appraisal is based on an infinite scale. It never changes with time or bends to others' classifications. He sees our intrinsic value now and the person we have the potential to become. He always has and always will. Because of what He suffered for us, His viewpoint matters more than anyone else's. He wouldn't want us to let our own limited estimation or the opinions of anyone else make us feel less than we actually are.

In a seminar my husband attended for work, the presenter said we often see our future based on what has happened in the past. Sometimes that view doesn't offer the brightest outlook or bolster our sense of worth, because as mortals (especially female ones), we have the tendency to focus on our failures and shortcomings. If we have sinned or made mistakes—and we all have—because of Jesus Christ, we don't have to see ourselves or our future that way. He gave

13 Margery Stockseth, "He Thought of Me," *New Era*, Apr. 1985, 51.
14 Camille Fronk, *Living the Young Women Values*, (Salt Lake City: Bookcraft, 1999), 25. Used with permission.

everything for us to live, choose, and progress on this earth. He gave us the ability to repent and move on. Though His sacrifice and suffering were wrought centuries ago, His gift to us isn't just an event that happened anciently. When we let it influence and shape our lives, the power of the Atonement is as new and every bit as real and transforming and restorative today as it was in His day.

Restoration is a powerful word, but it is even more powerful in action. It is the return of something to an unimpaired condition, the restitution of something taken away or lost, and is the promise of what the Savior will do for us. We read in Joel 2:25, "And I will restore to you the years that the locust hath eaten." Jesus Christ can and does restore us personally when we have sinned or don't feel whole, for whatever reason. It is a great blessing, filled with hopefulness, that in all our losses and in our difficulty here on earth, there will ultimately be restoration because of Him.

It is amazing to consider that something or someone in any state of disrepair can be made whole again and just like new. The restoration process is the biggest reason I love to watch home improvement shows. I'm often awestruck by the change that occurs that I would never have envisioned. While I love personal home improvement projects a little less, I took on a small restoration project with one of my great-grandmother Carson's old kitchen chairs. My mom gave it to my oldest daughter, Whitney, and we both talked for the longest time about fixing it up. As weeks and months turned to years, the chair that had already been in rough shape was in pieces—pieces I wasn't sure I could put back together. Finally, the organizer in me made a decision that it was either fix it up or throw it out. And I couldn't throw it out, because of the intangible connection with my great-grandmother, whom I'd never met.

In the furniture restoration department, I rank amateur at best. I know there are experts who restore paintings and furniture and other priceless things all the time. I couldn't afford to consult a professional for my project, so I rolled up my sleeves, pulled out my sander, and went to work. I probably broke a lot of cardinal rules about restoration, but after much effort, late nights, sweat, and even tears, I saved Grandma's chair. It's no longer in pieces all over my basement floor but is beautiful again and useful, as it once was.

It's hard not to see the similarities. Like the old chair, we can be made new when we are in pieces. Through Jesus Christ, if we are in disrepair or feel we are lacking for any reason, we are able to shed our natural selves, our lack of confidence, our sins, and our sorrows as His power restores us to what we were and makes of us an even better version of ourselves. Because of the Atonement, we have limitless possibilities and endless tomorrows, no matter what has happened before. The future is wide open. Armed with that knowledge, how would it be to grab hold of the worth Jesus Christ sees in us and never let it go?

Barbara Day Lockhart wrote, "Of all people on the earth, it makes the least sense for a Latter-day Saint to suffer from a poor self-image. We have been blessed to know the truth, and we have been given the opportunity to take that truth to all the world. How can we be a light to others if we are trapped in mists of insecurity and self-doubt? As we love Christ, have faith in him, desire to be like him, and follow him, he will change us, perfect us, and ultimately bring us home."[15]

Believing and relying on what the Savior did for us and how He feels about us can help us shed the insecurities that cause us to doubt ourselves. His love and gift of Atonement can help us leave past mistakes behind that weigh us down or hold us back. We can live life to the fullest and embrace our value based on the inestimable, unchanging price He paid. As we do, we gain the confidence to focus less on our imperfections and more on what our Savior desires to help us become—confident, faithful, powerful women of God, secure in His love, in our own worth, and in our individual missions as daughters of a loving Father, joint heirs with Jesus Christ.

15 Barbara Day Lockhart, "Our Divinely Based Worth," *Ensign*, Jun. 1995, 51.

Chapter Three
I Am Thankful for Fish

God Himself said we are the reason He created the universe! . . . [T]he vast expanse of eternity, the glories and mysteries of infinite space and time are all built for the benefit of ordinary mortals like you and me.[16] —Dieter F. Uchtdorf

MANY YEARS AGO, WHEN THE course of study for Relief Society centered on the teachings of President Brigham Young, I was an instructor in my ward. It was my first time teaching Relief Society, and I relished the opportunity the personal preparation gave me to study and learn things I had never known before. As much as I loved that calling, some of the lessons were far more challenging for me to understand and teach than others.

One Saturday evening, I was frantically finishing one of those lessons that was difficult for me. The subject was the Atonement. I'd been reading and studying the manual for several weeks, but right at that moment, nothing about my outline or my teaching ability seemed adequate for such a transcendent topic. I started doubting myself to the point that I was convinced the lesson would certainly be a disaster. At first I tried to be reasonable. I reminded myself that it was late and that I'm famous for overexaggerating at night the things that always seem clearer in the light of day. When that didn't help, I panicked. (If you've ever tried to receive inspiration in that frame of mind, you probably have a good idea of how the rest of the evening went.)

On the same Saturday evening, my husband was finishing up a lesson as well. We both snuck away to the same quiet spot to study. We worked side by side for a while without speaking. I was getting nowhere fast. In need of a break, I finally breached the silence and jokingly asked if he would also be teaching the Atonement to his nursery class. He nonchalantly replied that his schedule specified lesson eleven: "I Am Thankful for Fish." He also disclosed his plans to

16 Dieter F. Uchtdorf, "You Matter to Him," *Ensign*, Nov. 2011, 20.

use our nifty fishing bucket and pole, which I'd never brought to Relief Society but was a favorite in every Primary class I'd ever taught. To add insult to injury, he lamented that it was going to be a tough one to teach. We both laughed and my mood improved, but I really wished the message of the lesson I was going to give the next day was that simple to teach and understand.

Shortly after I gave that lesson on the Atonement (which wasn't quite the disaster I had envisioned), I took the opportunity to thumb through the orange Primary 1 manual. I had taught Primary many times, but never in nursery. I was touched by what I found there. Along with the aforementioned lesson on fish, there were lessons on animals, birds, insects, water, trees, plants, and flowers. The material was tailored for toddlers, so it was simple and straightforward. It was easy to see how the reinforcement in class could foster tiny testimonies as the children learned that our Heavenly Father and Jesus Christ made the fish, the birds, the trees, and many other wonderful things for them.

The lesson also brought to mind a remarkable scripture extolling the work of the Creation. In essence, the simple "I Am Thankful for Fish" was another way of saying, "Let the mountains shout for joy, and all ye valleys cry aloud; and all ye seas and dry lands tell the wonders of your Eternal King! And ye rivers, and brooks, and rills, flow down with gladness. Let the woods and all the trees of the field praise the Lord; and ye solid rocks weep for joy! And let the sun, moon, and the morning stars sing together, and let all the sons of God shout for joy! And let the eternal creations declare his name forever and ever!" (D&C 128:23).

Amen! And let us never forget that the Creation of our world and all that is on it is another significant piece of God's wondrous work in our behalf. This mortal proving ground didn't have to be as lovely as it is, but God's attention to detail and the world's resultant grandeur points directly to His love for us.

It's easy to see His power in a rolling thunderstorm, snow-encrusted mountaintops, or massive waves crashing against a rugged shore. It's humbling to see His gentle hand in the soothing melody of a mountain stream, in the perfection of a flower petal, and in the countless combinations of fish in the ocean or birds in the sky. It's astonishing to consider that even snowflakes fall to earth in equally delicate and unending patterns. We are awed and inspired by the vision and limitlessness of it all!

A past visiting teaching message presented the very idea that we *are* the reason God created the world and all its wonders. On a visit with one of our sisters, my companion beautifully conveyed the message. Afterward, the sister we visited shared some of her thoughts with us. She said she had wondered many times if Heavenly Father had made a specific flower in a certain color because He knew she liked that color. The thought ran through me like a breath of fresh air. It was nice to consider the Creation of this vast planet on such a personal level.

Several years ago, I had an experience that helped me understand that a bunch of pelicans were here just for me, at least for a season. I first noticed them on the pond close to my home during an especially difficult autumn. My husband became aware of them around the same time. Since we knew very little about birds of any variety, we weren't sure what they were. After conducting an Internet search and later consulting a friend and amateur ornithologist, we agreed that the strange creatures on the pond were indeed pelicans. After all, we were pretty sure we had also seen some in the zoo.

I often wondered what a bunch of crazy pelicans was doing in the middle of a pond in northern Utah. They seemed exotic to me, and I guess I expected them to frequent more exotic locales. I always pointed them out to my children, who were a captive audience in my van. (They thought I was crazy, but most of the time they smiled and nodded as though they were really paying attention.)

Just prior to the arrival of the pelicans, our family had run into a series of obstacles that seemed insurmountable and had left me searching for peace. As I darted from one place to another—work, errands, picking up and delivering children—it thrilled me that part of my journey usually meant passing by them. Sometimes, when I could snatch a few moments out of a busy morning, I would stop briefly by the side of the road and count their growing numbers. Often, I counted sixty or more from a group that had begun with just three or four.

I don't know how to explain it, but observing the pelicans gave me solace at a time when peace seemed especially elusive. They became a symbol of hope. Whenever I saw them, I felt more deeply of my Father's awareness of me than I ever had before. I even referred to them as "mine." I knew they were a gift from heaven I couldn't and shouldn't ignore. It might sound silly, but they really were the difference for me in navigating that difficult time. I saw God's hand and His love for me in the pelicans.

Evidence of God's love is in His handiwork all around us. All we need to do is look. A dear friend of mine wrote of a tender experience she had with her son as he saw Heavenly Father's love for him in the stars:

> In a moment labeled
> "Quality time,"
> I gaze with you at the stars.

Your little-boy excitement
Tugs at my heart
While thoughts
Of Copernicus and Galileo
Lend me a moment to
Teach.
So I ask,
"How do they stay in the sky?"
Then my tears send the stars swimming
In a misty kaleidoscope
As you teach me
With your
Faith:
"I think
Heavenly Father
Glues them
To the clouds."[17]

It was such a sweet and earnest sentiment—not of a fanciful expression of an imaginary event—coming from a believing child who had no doubt that God would have taken the time to paste by hand the millions of stars to the clouds just for him to enjoy. Even though our Heavenly Father surely employed other methods in creating the glorious spectacle that is the night sky, however He did it, however long it took, there is no doubt He made it happen for us.

It's no wonder we feel closer to God when we are close to the things He created for us, nor is it a stretch to feel His love and our value in them. There is nothing quite like being at one with the resplendence of a world around us that greets our eyes and warms our senses every single day. A simple hymn entitled "God's Daily Care" gently suggests a message of love inspired by a sunrise. Congregations sing it all the time, but I'd never really paid attention to it until I sang it recently with the rest of my ward family. I felt like I'd heard it for the first time, and I was stirred by the message:

As I watch the rising sun
When the day has just begun,
I am thinking of the love
That comes daily from above.[18]

17 Vicki B. Wright, "Of Things Scientific," *Ensign*, Feb. 1998, 61.
18 "God's Daily Care," *Hymns*, no. 306.

Doesn't God's love warm us like the sun and sustain us? Doesn't it come to us daily, hourly, or even minute to minute if that's the way we need it? We can see it, touch it, smell it, and taste it in the world around us. We can also feel it in our hearts as we remember that our Savior, Jesus Christ, under the direction of our Father in Heaven, created the fish, the birds, the flowers, the trees, and so many other magnificent things—just for us.

Chapter Four
Is This Trip Really Necessary?

The personal value, the sacred splendor of every one of you, is the very reason there is a plan for salvation and exaltation.[19] —Jeffrey R. Holland

THERE ARE THEORIES ABOUNDING ABOUT how life on this earth began and where we all go after it ends. Some say the world magically came to be as the result of a great cosmic accident or that humans evolved from another species. Others believe there is nothing in space but space and that after we die we return to the earth, so what we do here makes no difference at all. Conversely, we believe we are here for a purpose and are an integral part of a glorious plan without beginning or end. Though our finite minds can't comprehend it completely, a tenet of our faith and a guiding force in our lives is that our ultimate quest is to be reunited with God, the author of the plan of salvation. We know from revelation that we are the reason there is a plan in the first place.

If my memory serves me correctly, when I was just a young girl, a sign appeared on the door of a friend's home as one school year ended. It read simply, *Is this trip really necessary?* I had no idea then that it was meant for us. In fact, I don't think I really understood the question it posed until I spent a few summers as a grown-up with my own children out of school.

Summer days back then were different than they are today. My best friends and I spent many carefree hours playing outside together. We often gathered with other neighborhood friends for never-ending games of baseball or kick the can. There were also other simple pleasures we enjoyed, like lemonade sales, backyard theatrical productions, and basketball games in the driveway. With all the energy we expended, sometimes we got hungry or thirsty or hot, which meant that several times a day, we would traipse through my house or a friend's house in search of a snack or a place to cool off. I'm sure now that the

19 Jeffrey R. Holland, "Because of Your Faith," *Ensign*, Nov. 2010, 6.

Is this trip really necessary? sign was prompted by the constant stream of bare feet and the slamming of the screen door. It was simply a strategic preemptive strike, another way of asking, "Do you really need another glass of punch?" "Are you sure you have to use the bathroom again?" I don't think the sign ever stopped us or even gave us pause. Of course those trips were necessary! We wouldn't have made them if they weren't.

In the heat of a difficult moment or awash in a stream of unfulfilled expectations, have you ever asked yourself if *this* trip is really necessary—the one we made to earth? In the thick of hectic schedules and pressure-packed situations, have you entertained the idea that you must have been standing in the back of heaven chatting with friends or simply not paying attention during that grand council when it was all laid out before us? The scriptures tell us that not only did we know about our Heavenly Father's plan before we were born but we were also happy about it. In fact, we shouted for joy (see Job 38:7). It makes perfect sense that our God of order has a plan for each of us. Evidenced by our mortal birth, we happily chose His plan in our premortal life, and we have the agency to choose His plan for us here.

Most of the time I think I viewed the plan of salvation as steps on a chart like the ones we've all seen in Primary or Sunday School. It's instructive to understand it that way, but our Heavenly Father's plan is also more simply put. It is the gospel of Jesus Christ. He marked the way for us. While the way to eternal life is straight and narrow (see 2 Ne. 31:19), mortal life is not a one-size-fits-all proposition. Our experiences here are varied and our opportunities are unique. By divine design, within the all-encompassing plan of salvation, there are also individual plans for each of us. Indeed, as Elder Neal A. Maxwell said, "God is in the details of our lives."[20]

I don't know about you, but I like a good plan. Sometimes, to my detriment, I'm an advocate of the old saying, "If you fail to plan, you plan to fail." I especially prefer it when things go exactly according to *my* plan. If you've lived here for a while, you probably know how that approach has worked out for me. It always seems like the plans for our days that allow for the completion of essential tasks and responsibilities are disrupted by a schedule change, a minor disaster, or a more pressing need. It happens every day. Even though these types of changes might make us grumble and are temporarily frustrating, they generally can be easily adapted to with a moderate amount of effort and aggravation. On a larger scale, life is unpredictable at best, and there are going to be some bigger bumps in the road than minor schedule changes. It's the big plans we have for ourselves and our lives that we sometimes have to yield when God has other plans for

---

20 Neal A. Maxwell, "Becoming a Disciple," *Ensign*, Jun. 1996, 12.

us. When we put our trust in Him, we won't be thrown completely off balance or abandon our beliefs, because we are able to keep sight of His great plan, no matter what we are called to pass through.

In Primary, the children often sing these simple words with a profound message: "I will follow God's plan for me."[21] The message of the song centers on developing the kind of faith that allows us to accept that it's God's plans, not our own, that will get us where He wants us to be. Our will is the only thing that is truly ours to give, so we must learn to let go, give ourselves to Him, and trust His plan for us, even when it's a difficult journey.

One of my favorite hobbies is sewing. Since my talent for design is limited, I almost always use a pattern. I've learned through the years that there are some key elements to the success of a sewing project for me. The first thing I *should* do with a pattern, prior to any cutting or stitching, is read the instructions, exactly as the pattern company suggests. I always do that when I'm not in a hurry, which is practically never. Usually I dive right in only to regret it in the end because it almost invariably means unpicking mistakes or even starting over. If you don't sew, you may be wondering why that is. The instructions include helpful, general sewing terms and critical information unique to that pattern. One of the most important tidbits refers to the seam allowance. The customary seam for most projects is five-eighths of an inch. Imagine finishing a project only to discover that it doesn't fit or is a miniature version of the expected result because the instructions specified a smaller seam and you missed it because you didn't read them. A little variance doesn't sound like a lot, but it can make a big difference when applied to an entire project.

There are other helpful tips included in the instructions, like the pattern layout and cutting guide, seam trimming, and length adjustment. Sounds like riveting reading, doesn't it? While it doesn't have the intrigue of a suspenseful mystery novel or an interesting magazine article, reading and following the instructions is essential. Even if it seems a little restrictive with all those steps, there is plenty of room for creativity. I don't have to choose the same fabric or trim that is rendered on the pattern envelope. Pockets, buttons, and other embellishments can be added where there are none. Hemlines can be changed, along with lots of other little touches if I prefer. The most important thing I've learned through the years about sewing is that if I skip steps or ignore the basics, I usually end up frustrated and dissatisfied with the final result.

And so it goes with our lives. The purpose of life has been unfolded and laid out before us in a marvelously detailed yet understandable way. It is our Father's plan, and Jesus Christ set the pattern for us to follow. Understanding

---

21 "I Will Follow God's Plan," *Children's Songbook*, 164–65.

and following the plan of happiness enables us to experience the type of success we would never attain if we chose to ignore His instructions and go it entirely on our own. God's pattern gives us direction and meaning as we govern our lives. It also enables us to recognize our vital role in building up His kingdom on this earth. He designed all of it to enable us to receive a body, to live and learn, and to find our way back to Him.

We may wonder, as the Psalmist did, "When I consider thy heavens, the work of thy fingers, the moon and the stars, which thou hast ordained; what is man, that thou art mindful of him? and the son of man, that thou visitest him?" (Ps. 8:3–4).

And we stand in awe at the remarkable answer. "For thou hast made him a little lower than the angels, and hast crowned him with glory and honour" (Ps. 8:5).

President Dieter F. Uchtdorf expounded further, "Compared to God, man is nothing; yet we are everything to God. While against the backdrop of infinite creation we may appear to be nothing, we have a spark of eternal fire burning within our breast. We have the incomprehensible promise of exaltation—worlds without end—within our grasp. And it is God's great desire to help us reach it."[22]

It's good to know that in this great big world, our Heavenly Father has something infinite in mind for each of us. His plan gives meaning and purpose to the choices we make and the paths we choose. Our eternal life, or the life that He lives, is His work and glory (see Moses 1:39). Like any other loving parent, He wants us to succeed splendidly. As an inspired stake president said when he set my son-in-law apart for a calling, "All of God's greatest glories come from our successes."[23]

Life on this earth is just another stage, another step in His plan. God, who put His plan into motion eternities ago, is mindful of us. Our journey here is a testament of His love for us. In moments of apprehension or frustration, when we wonder if this trip is really necessary, the answer is a resounding yes! Mortal life, with its trials, triumphs, heartaches, and happiness, is all part of His glorious plan for us and our only way back to Him!

---

22 Dieter F. Uchtdorf, "You Matter to Him," *Ensign*, Nov. 2011, 20.
23 Personal notes in possession of the author.

Chapter Five
You Are Not a Winner. Try Again!

My dear sisters, your Heavenly Father loves you—each of you. That love never changes. It is not influenced by your appearance, by your possessions, or by the amount of money you have in your bank account. It is not changed by your talents and abilities. It is simply there. It is there for you when you are sad or happy, discouraged or hopeful. God's love is there for you whether or not you feel you deserve love. It is simply always there.[24] —Thomas S. Monson

AFTER WAITING IN THE WINGS for centuries, it is our opportunity to live during the last days on this earth. In spite of all we understand about who we are and why we matter so much, it would be naïve to suggest that we aren't ever going to have some difficult days or periods of time when our confidence wanes and we feel less than we are.

What can cause us to lose sight of our eternal worth and mission? The short list might include the hurtful opinions or actions of others, trials and challenges we face, our own sins, mistakes and shortcomings, unhappiness, envy, and dissatisfaction. Many years ago, a silly candy bar wrapper prompted me to ask some important questions about how I viewed myself and what I was allowing to dictate how I felt about me.

At the end of a very long day, I may or may not have been feeling sorry for myself when I reached into the pantry for something to eat. I'm usually drawn to salty foods like popcorn or potato chips for my consolation snacks, so I surprised myself when I chose a piece of chocolate. Since I was home alone, I didn't have to share my treat with anyone else, and I planned to enjoy every sugary bite. I've long forgotten the reason for the negative feelings that day, but I do remember settling into the couch cushions and casually opening the wrapper. What I didn't realize until I peeled away the package was that the candy bar in my hands was part of a fantastic prize giveaway.

24 Thomas S. Monson, "We Never Walk Alone," *Ensign*, Nov. 2013, 123–24.

Please know that I had read Roald Dahl's *Charlie and the Chocolate Factory* more than once in my youth and had watched the movie adaptation starring Gene Wilder with my children at least a hundred times. (That might sound like an exaggeration, but I'm pretty sure it's close since they have almost every line memorized and can still recite them on demand even though they're grown.) Charlie and his quest for the golden ticket was the first thing that came to my mind as I anticipated my current participation in this new and exciting candy bar contest. For just a tiny moment, I imagined all the possibilities. What would I do if I won a tropical vacation, the car of my dreams, or a tidy bundle of cash? Even a trip to a candy factory would mean a welcome respite from my usual task list, as long as I didn't turn into a giant blueberry or get stuck in a tube filled with chocolate. (Don't get me wrong, I love chocolate; I just prefer not to drown in it.) I could almost picture myself accepting the grand prize, whatever it was. Alas, those happy thoughts didn't last long. As I slid my thumb under the seam and opened the package, what I saw written boldly inside told me immediately that this candy bar didn't contain a golden ticket or anything even close. Instead, the message only echoed my current estimation of myself and glared up at me: *Sorry, you are not a winner. Try again!*

Though the message wasn't quite as harsh as calling me a loser, it was practically the same thing. Normally I would have disregarded the wrapper and continued on to the chocolate, but the words stopped me in my tracks. Why? As I read them, I realized I had been telling myself exactly the same thing over and over, minus the more positive *try again* part. For weeks, I'd been struggling with feelings of inadequacy and self-doubt. What had I really accomplished in my life? What did I have to offer? It seemed to me that my contributions hadn't measured up to my self-imposed rigorous estimation of success, and now that uncaring candy wrapper reminded me of what I already knew.

The irony of that experience was not lost on me. Now, the wrapper didn't really make me feel bad. I knew, for many reasons, it didn't make any sense to take the message to heart or to even give it a second thought. The chocolate maker and the contest promoter knew nothing about me. They didn't know (or care) how I was feeling. They had no idea of the decisions I'd made, good or bad. They weren't aware of my hopes and dreams. It would be ridiculous to suggest that the words were personal, but in a moment of reflection, I had to admit that sometimes I do listen to messages concerning my worth from sources that don't have any more right to comment than the candy wrapper did. Maybe you do too.

As we go through our lives, we are going to receive many different types of messages, most of which will have a greater impact for good or ill than the one tucked inside that candy bar. Some will be spoken, others will not. Some will be said to us directly and others might go on behind our backs. Some will come from those around us, others from television, movies, magazines, or though social media. Some are unintentional, and how we take them is more a reflection of how we feel about ourselves than anything else. Others are more personal and might shake us to the core. What happens when we wrap ourselves in the negative messages we see and hear? If we let them stay and settle in and become a part of us, we begin to doubt what we know about the eternal nature of our worth, which could lead us to question ourselves and our own unique contributions. As we do, we become less confident and less effective in our lives.

If we're paying attention, we also receive many warm and wonderful messages in word and deed from people in our lives—actions of acceptance, affirmations of love and gratitude, and words of hope, faith, encouragement, and concern. I suspect that if we counted them, the positive would far outweigh the unfavorable. However, even with all the good, we often record and recall the negative more clearly. I have found in my own life that from the numerous comments I receive, I remember longer, more intensely, and take more to heart the one that is negative than the one that is positive and uplifting.

I don't know the reason for it, but it reminds me of something that happens when toddlers are first learning to talk. They hear hundreds, maybe even thousands, of perfectly appropriate words. It's a phenomenon of toddlerhood, much to a parent's dismay, that young children often remember and repeat the unfortunate words they've heard only once, and not only that, but they let them slip from their mouths at the most inconvenient times, like at church, family parties, and other social functions where they have a maximum impact. In a similar way, we hold tighter to the unflattering thoughts about ourselves or the careless actions of others that hurt us rather than the hundreds of lovely things that uplift our souls and speak of our worth. For some reason, it's the negative that sticks. While it's certainly human to hold on to the disparaging messages we hear, it is hazardous to our self-worth to let them linger in our minds and hearts. Likewise, as we're addressing the negative impact hurtful words from others can make, we must also be aware that it's not only what comes from the outside that affects us. The most familiar voice and harshest criticism often comes from within.

What do you say when you talk to yourself? Do you cheer yourself on when you make a mistake, or do you have a hard time giving yourself a break but bend over backward to see the best in everyone else? Do you ever tell yourself you're not good enough, talented enough, pretty enough, smart enough? There is nothing wrong with expecting the best of ourselves and doing our best. But our best is just that—ours. We get into trouble when we expect too much and then pile on the guilt when we either don't meet all our expectations, or the execution of our efforts is less than what we'd hoped. Our worth is not based on performance or perfection. Remember, we brought it with us. Even though we are not perfect, we are enough!

When we entertain self-defeating thoughts, rest assured they are not coming from our Heavenly Father or our Savior, Jesus Christ. They come from the adversary, who has a different agenda for us entirely. He relishes the opportunity to exploit our discouragement and self-doubt for his own purposes. He wants to get us off course. That's easier for him when we get discouraged or lose faith in ourselves. Ann, a wise and wonderful Relief Society president in my ward, shared an enlightening idea. To paraphrase, she passed along an idea she'd read that the negative way we speak to ourselves isn't just self-talk but the adversary talking to us in our own voice,[25] which was a stunning realization to me! It seems so obvious the need to filter out the messages coming from him, but since we're used to hearing our own voice, we may not recognize the words we say to ourselves for what they are. Identifying the source of those messages enables us to more easily detect and eliminate them.

For illustrative purposes, Ann also invited us to take a minute to list some things we don't like about ourselves. After our time was up, she noted how easy it seemed for the vast majority of us. Afterward, also at her invitation, we wrote a different list of things we think we do well. As you might suspect, the second list of strengths was much harder for most of us to make. While it's fine to take note of ways we want to improve and changes we can make, too often we focus more on what we aren't than on what we are in a self-defeating way that doesn't promote anything good or productive.

I have a helpful tip. Have you ever tried to talk to a teenager when he or she has headphones on? My son wears them all the time because he apparently does his best work to musical accompaniment. He claims the headphones help him concentrate. I don't know if they do or if they don't, but I've accepted the fact that there is nothing getting past those devices and into listening ears, no matter how loud or significant the message. When he wears them, I usually have to jump up and down or wave my arms like a flagman during road construction to get his attention. However, when considering messages that tear us down or cause us to question ourselves, we should be exactly like my son with his incredible noise-blocking headphones—tune the negative messages out, shut them down, let them go, or, better yet, pretend we don't hear them at all!

25 See Maurice W. Harker, *Like Dragons Did They Fight: A Synergy of Eternal Principles and Accurate Science for Personal Self-Mastery,* 2nd ed. (Maurice W. Harker, 2017), 17.

We make progress on the path to self-acceptance when we refuse to define ourselves by the labels of the world or by our shortcomings, weaknesses, or mistakes. I hope you will never be the recipient of the kind of message tucked inside my candy bar that day. But if you ever do feel or hear that you are not a winner, please believe that a loving Father sent you to earth wrapped gently in His love and in your real worth—a definition that is honest and lasting and comes from being His child.

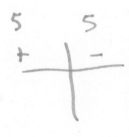

Chapter Six
The Parable of the Pantyhose

We are conscious of our weaknesses, but we know the Lord can use those very weaknesses to bless our lives and that through Him . . . our weaknesses can become strengths.[26] —Glenn L. Pace

IT'S NO SECRET THAT NONE of us is perfect. We all fall short of the mark. But even with the understanding that perfection is a process that's going to take more than a lifetime, we're often disappointed when we're less than perfect here. Sometimes what we perceive about those imperfections, real or imagined, can cause us to question our worth. It's an absolute truth that our imperfections and weaknesses don't change our value at all. Being human, faults and flaws are part of who we are. That being said, it's not uncommon for us to let our shortcomings outweigh what we know about ourselves and fill us with discouragement and self-doubt. Who knew that a run in a pair of pantyhose could help me see my flaws in a completely different way?

After a day of frantic errand-running and taking care of other responsibilities, I had only about fifteen minutes to make myself presentable for a seven o'clock church meeting. With the clock ticking and me running out of time, I quickly reached into my closet and pulled out my trusty black suit. It had never failed me before. Though I'd bought it on clearance when I was looking for something else, it turned out to be one of my all-time favorite purchases. As I slipped it on that evening, like a mere mortal stepping into a phone booth and coming out a superhero, I hoped it had power to transform me again.

Hurried and running out of time, I rummaged around in my drawer looking for a pair of pantyhose without a run in them. Going in, I knew it was a feat that could not be taken lightly. To my great surprise, I quickly found a pair that seemed to be in pretty good shape. I sighed with relief in a mini moment of

26 Glenn L. Pace, "Confidence and Self-Worth," *Ensign*, Jan. 2005, 32.

triumph. (It's amazing how such small things can feel like big accomplishments on crazy days.) *Maybe I can make it to the meeting on time*, I thought, suddenly hopeful. I frantically brushed my teeth, ran a brush through my hair, and touched up my makeup. Finally, all I needed was to put on my shoes before I was on my way. When I slipped my feet into my black pumps one at a time, I nearly jumped when I saw the run I hadn't noticed when I first pulled my pantyhose on. I don't know how in the world I missed it. It was huge, starting somewhere around my big toe and ending who knows where.

The gigantic run prompted a sudden insecurity, even in my black suit. I wondered if I dared wear them to the church meeting in that condition or if I should go at all since I knew I didn't have another pair. "Go without them," you say? "No one wears pantyhose anymore anyway." You are absolutely right! Due to the lack of selection in the stores these days, I'm fully aware I'm one of the last women on the planet to cling to my pantyhose. But that's not going to change anytime soon. If I'm being honest, it's because I feel bad about my bare legs. They almost always need more sun and usually a shave. They could also be more toned, and my heels are a mess, but I digress. There was simply no time to address those concerns, and I knew there was no way I could stop to buy another pair and make the meeting on time. And walking in late seemed worse to me than going to the meeting with a giant run in my hose.

At that point, I had to address my options. I contemplated missing the meeting entirely and just staying home. It *had* been a long day. On the other hand, staying home from a meeting due to a run in some pantyhose didn't seem remotely like a legitimate excuse, especially to someone who would feel guilty about it for years. In the end, I decided my dilemma made very little difference in the eternal scheme of things. Besides, I needed the spiritual boost the meeting would provide. I took one last look in the mirror and hoped no one would notice, knowing full well they couldn't help but see the run that was so large it practically announced its presence.

As I was driving to the church that evening, the problem with my stockings prompted thoughts about other imperfections that have less to do with pantyhose and more to do with shortcomings brought on by mortal weakness. Everyone has them, even when we think we are alone in all our faults and failings. And especially when we wonder how others could possibly miss those pesky traits that often seem large and conspicuous to us, like a giant run in a pair of hose.

There are reasons for our imperfections. We stumble and fall sometimes because we are human and we have agency. As you'll recall, it was Satan's plan to force us to make all the right decisions, to never make mistakes. It's not revelatory or groundbreaking news that we will not be perfect here. God's plan allows us to choose for ourselves, to have joy and sorrow, to understand the good from the bad, to experience triumphs and trials, to make mistakes, and to have imperfections.

Before we get too carried away talking about our weaknesses, consider this remarkable thought by Elder L. Tom Perry. "One of the greatest weaknesses in most of us is our lack of faith in ourselves. One of our common failings is to depreciate our tremendous worth."[27] Perhaps we should stick that thought on our foreheads and wear it around so we see it every time we look in the mirror and never forget.

Being preoccupied with our faults isn't productive, especially when we focus so much on what we aren't that it keeps us from discovering who we are. While we might wish we didn't have weaknesses, overcoming them can turn us to God and foster personal growth. If we could do everything perfectly well on our own, we would certainly not rely on Him for guidance and sustenance, or at least not as much as we should. As we travel the road to becoming the best version of ourselves, a loving God has generously offered His help. If we come to Him when we want to change, He will help us and support and inspire us as we work to turn our weaknesses into strengths (see Ether 12:27).

It's funny to me now, but as a young girl and even into early adulthood, I believed I could be perfect—in this life. I'm not kidding! I thought that if I was good enough, worked hard enough, and was faithful enough, I could be practically, if not completely, perfect in every way in mortality, not unlike the fictional Mary Poppins. It's not that I was unaware of the debt of gratitude I owe my Savior and can never repay. I stand in awe of Him, of all He has done, and of all He continues to do for me every day. I did then as well. The idea was actually born of a desire to be good, to love and serve Him with everything I had so as not to be responsible for any more than my share of His heartrending suffering. The result? I wasn't perfect. I'm still not. In fact, I'm not even close. And in the quest for perfection, I was unduly impatient and incredibly hard on myself when I made mistakes, even small ones. I had trouble forgiving myself. I misunderstood what willpower and discipline could accomplish. I hadn't applied the most vital part of the equation: I need my Savior desperately. We all do! Out of love for Him, we do all we can, and then we are made perfect through the Atonement of Jesus Christ.

Make no mistake about it; God wants us to be like He is. We read it in the scriptures. "Be ye therefore perfect, even as your Father which is in heaven is perfect" (Matt. 5:48). The scriptures also speak of the learning process in

27 L. Tom Perry, "Be the Best of Whatever You Are" (Brigham Young University devotional, Mar. 12, 1974); speeches.byu.edu.

mortality as line upon line, precept upon precept, here a little, there a little, not everything at once (see Isa. 28:10). We achieve perfection a step at a time, just like we attain knowledge and experience. That process will continue in the life beyond this. We will not be perfect here, no matter how hard we try or how devoted we are, because we are human and we are going to make mistakes. In fulfilling our various roles and doing our part, our Heavenly Father asks that we do our best and press on without letting our weaknesses discourage us to the point of giving up. We will need patience in our imperfections and the persistence to try and try again.

President Uchtdorf said:

> Sometimes we feel discouraged because we are not "more" of something—more spiritual, respected, intelligent, healthy, rich, friendly, or capable. Naturally, there is nothing wrong with wanting to improve. God created us to grow and progress. But remember, our weaknesses can help us to be humble and turn us to Christ, who will "make weak things become strong"[Ether 12:27]. . . .
>
> I learned in my life that we don't need to be "more" of anything to start to become the person God intended us to become.[28]

President Uchtdorf's advice on the process of perfecting ourselves reminds me of some instructions I've heard a time or two while practicing yoga. I work out to a few simple DVDs I've used over and over again through the years. I've come to enjoy the soothing voice of one instructor as he reminds me that in my practice I should focus on working hard without pressuring myself to be perfect. He has nothing to worry about. There will never be a day I will be perfect at yoga, and I know it. (He'd know it too if he could see me.) His good advice for yoga practice is even better advice for life. It wouldn't be a bad motto to carry with us all the time.

One of my favorite positions in yoga is a balancing posture called the airplane. From a simple standing pose, both arms are extended out to the side. The pose is completed by leaning forward, hips square, and slowly lifting one leg off the ground behind while the standing leg is firm. Both arms are then brought out to each side. It might look simple written in those few instructions. It's not. At least it's not for me. I wobble a lot and fall out of the pose frequently, but I

---

28 Dieter F. Uchtdorf, "It Works Wonderfully!" *Ensign*, Nov. 2015, 22.

keep trying. As I practice regularly, I feel more stable, stronger, and more confident. Eventually I may even be able to hold the pose for an extended period of
time.

In yoga and in life, it's easy to lose our balance. Sometimes we find there's
too much of this and not enough of that, and the combination makes us
unsteady. Often our expectations don't meet our results, which can also throw
us off-kilter. Thus, the advice to extend a sincere effort without the pressure of
perfection is something we can strive to implement that enables better balance
in all the aspects of our complicated lives.

In my humble opinion, the biggest problem we as women face is not
usually an unawareness of our faults and failings, but exactly the opposite: a
hyperawareness. We often see them just like I saw that run in my pantyhose—
glaringly large and practically impossible to miss. What adds to the trouble is
that we don't look at our faults and weaknesses with the naked eye; we tend
to see them through a magnifying glass, so they seem hairier and scarier and
much more prominent than they really are. In spite of those tendencies, in
coming to God in our weakness, we are humbly submitting. We are asking
Him to help us identify what we need to work on and what weaknesses we can
eliminate that will help us become what He wants us to be.

The first step is the acknowledgment to our Maker that we can and want
to do better and that we can't do it all on our own. After we express the desire
for change, if we truly desire to change, we must then accept the opportunities
for transformation that come along. Those opportunities are going to get
uncomfortable. Growth usually is. Making changes will stretch us and test us
and cause us to honestly evaluate where we are and what is required to make
the necessary improvements. I found that out the hard way.

Years ago, it bothered me that I wasn't very patient. I admired the patient
people in my life and wanted to be like them. I expressed this desire to my
Heavenly Father. You can probably guess what happened. I found an abundance
of opportunities to learn patience with myself, with my family, with other
people, and with life's experiences that didn't unfold exactly the way I would
have liked. Believe it or not, I was surprised by the turn of events. Silly me. I
naïvely expected that God would grant me patience in the same way a fairy
godmother might grant a wish by waving her magic wand. I'd read about King
Solomon from ancient days, who was blessed with wisdom, and wondered
if the same type of thing might happen in the blink of an eye for me. While
I was earnest in my desire, the experience taught me that I would have to
learn it and earn it one patience-promoting experience at a time. More closely

examined, Solomon's wisdom probably didn't instantly appear either. It may have been a gift that was carefully developed and added to over time. Whether we desire more patience, increased faith, greater wisdom, or anything else, it holds true for all of us that our weaknesses do not go away without effort any more than the strengths we desire are developed overnight.

How do we acknowledge our weaknesses without letting them weigh us down or overtake us? How do we manage the feelings of inadequacy brought on by our humanness? We take it a little at a time. While there is no magic spell or quick and easy answer, there are some steps we can take on the path to being the very best version of ourselves.

Write your thoughts and goals: You may have already guessed that I'm old-fashioned. Even in a day of computer keyboards and virtual everything, I still believe in the power of writing things down with one of those pens or pencils on paper. There is something real and binding for me about seeing a goal or desire in black and white, written in my own hand. To amend the popular idiom, for me, the pen is more powerful than the keyboard. If writing something down doesn't give you any extra oomph, record your goal in whatever medium works best for you, and place it where you can see it easily and refer to it often. President Thomas S. Monson of the First Presidency stated, "When performance is measured, performance improves. When performance is measured and reported, the rate of improvement accelerates."[29] Recording objectives increases ownership and commitment much more than just contemplating them alone. Setting realistic dates and establishing timelines ensures accountability.

Set worthwhile goals, but be realistic: Identify your objective and follow that with short-term goals and the necessary steps required to reach them, building momentum on the improvement you've made. I love President Hinckley's advice to "try a little harder to be a little better."[30] Strive every day to try harder, but manage your expectations and don't anticipate reaching your destination all at once.

Acknowledge progress and celebrate strengths: In a friendly, youthful one-on-one basketball game with my best friend, I celebrated a shot I made that I personally thought belonged on the national highlight reels. In response to my shining moment, I shouted and jumped and cheered. I celebrated so much and annoyed my competitor enough that she commented, "Don't break your arm patting yourself on the back." We don't want to aggravate our fellow travelers

29 Thomas S. Monson, "How Do I Use My Time Wisely?" *Preach My Gospel: A Guide to Missionary Service* (2004), 150.
30 Gordon B. Hinckley, "We Have a Work to Do," *Ensign*, May 1995, 88.

with excessive celebration, but it's not going to hurt anything to congratulate ourselves for a job well done. Those acknowledgements can provide motivation to keep going.

Pray often. Ask for help: Since God has asked us to come to Him in our weakness, He isn't going to abandon us after He points them out. Prayer is an important part of everything we do, including overcoming weaknesses. We can always have a prayer in our hearts. Extra communication with our Heavenly Father, especially on days when reaching our goals seems more daunting, can give us the courage, strength, support, and insight we need to continue.

Have patience: Don't get discouraged. If you lose sight of your goals or get off track, start again. Forgive yourself. As President Hinckley reminded, "Please don't nag yourself with thoughts of failure."[31] There is always another day to look forward to, another opportunity to learn and grow and improve. Work to develop a hopeful optimism rather than giving in to self-defeating talk that only results in discouragement and often leads to the abandonment of the goal.

Remember, our imperfections do not make us worth less. They are not designed to overwhelm us or to cause us to give up. In the process of bettering ourselves, we would do well to keep in mind something President Dieter F. Uchtdorf said: "God loves you this very day and always. He is not waiting to love you until you have overcome your weaknesses and bad habits. He loves you today with a full understanding of your struggles."[32]

As we rely on our Heavenly Father for support, we strengthen the bond we have with Him, all the while gaining confidence in ourselves. His promise to help us is hopeful, and His love is unconditional. When it comes to our weaknesses, we must keep in mind the unchanging and remarkable truth—our Heavenly Father sees them all and loves us just the same.

How does understanding our eternal nature help us overcome insecurity and feelings of inadequacy and combat the messages that say something contrary to what we know from Church leaders, scripture, and personal affirmations from the Holy Ghost? It is everything! Our divinely based worth is the single most important consideration as we try to align the way we feel about ourselves in an unwavering way with who we really are. Additionally, some of the basic principles and practices of the gospel are essential tools in helping us maintain a steady sense of worth that is tied inseparably to how much we matter to our Father in Heaven. Just to be clear, there is nothing we

---

31 Gordon B. Hinckley, "Rise to the Stature of the Divine within You," *Ensign*, Nov. 1989, 96.

32 Dieter F. Uchtdorf, "Living the Gospel Joyful," *Ensign*, Nov. 2014, 123.

can do to increase our worth. It is already immeasurable. But in our real lives, feelings of self-worth often ebb and flow like the tide. Since our self-image relates to so many aspects of our lives, the next several chapters offer some suggestions we can implement as we all work to eliminate the ups and downs in an effort to ensure that our self-worth remains as constant as our real worth.

Chapter Seven
The Fine Print

Dear daughters of God, you are the crown jewels of all of His creations. . . . May
you catch the vision that you are destined to be a refined and regal queen, honored
by an uncountable posterity, worlds without end.[33] —Douglas L. Callister

IF YOU ENJOYED FAIRY TALES in your childhood, you may have imagined, like
I did, that life for you was going to be exactly like the stories on those pages.
Now that we've left our youth behind, we may find ourselves thinking that
except for a few brief moments here and there, our story may not read like
a fairy tale at all. The reality is that many of life's experiences might just fall
short of the magic in the charming storybook version of our dreams. Even so,
while we're here on earth writing our own story, remember that every story
has its ups and downs. (Think of poor Snow White and that trance-inducing
apple or the formerly long-haired Rapunzel and the reason for her short new
do.) Adapting to those ups and downs with our self-worth intact has a lot to
do with understanding (and even embracing) the fine print.

Several years ago, I was on a quest for the perfect birthday present for a
neighbor friend who was turning five. Since my own daughters were nearly
grown, I hadn't spent much time in the pink section of the toy store for a
while, and it was delightful! As I scoured the shelves for the perfect present, I
found a princess tracing desk. I knew right away it was the best of both worlds
for my young friend, since she happened to love drawing *and* princesses.

It wasn't until I took my purchase home and wrapped it that I noticed the
tiny disclaimer printed on one side of the box that read, *The actual item may*
not be identical to item pictured on the package. I was puzzled. How difficult was
it for the manufacturer to match the contents of the box with the picture on

---

33 Douglas L. Callister, "Your Refined Heavenly Home" (Brigham Young University devo-
    tional, Sept. 19, 2006); speeches.byu.edu.

the outside? Even as I pondered the possibilities, I realized that sometimes we might wonder about life in a similar context. Something like, *Your actual life may not be identical to the life you pictured.*

Perhaps our panoramic perspective in the premortal existence made life on earth seem more manageable than we sometimes find it here. After all, what are a few difficult moments in mortality compared to a glorious eternity, especially since we already had a taste of how grand it was going to be? Ironically, after we left the memory of that life behind, one of the biggest struggles of mortality is keeping it all in perspective.

Among the most poignant passages of scripture are those recorded by Joseph Smith, of his incarceration in Liberty Jail. The suffering of the Saints was clearly on the prophet's mind as he pleaded with Heavenly Father to divulge His hiding place and intervene in their behalf. Whenever I read those verses, knowing the hardship our faithful forbearers had already endured, I must admit I always wish the answer was different. I want their heartache, persecution, and privation to end. The heavenly reply to Joseph's anguished cries breaks my heart every time.

"My son, peace be unto thy soul; thine adversity and thine afflictions shall be but a small moment; and then, if thou endure it well, God shall exalt thee on high; thou shalt triumph over all thy foes" (D&C 121:7–8).

Because of God's omnipotence, He could have smoothed the way for all the early Saints. He could have also unloosed the bands of Joseph Smith's incarceration or even caused the prison walls to crumble as He had in ancient days. He could have made a path for Joseph's escape from what was yet to come. Instead, among all the messages our Heavenly Father might have shared with His faithful prophet, He tenderly offered perspective. He told Joseph not to fear, no matter what he was called to endure. He reminded him that Jesus Christ had suffered all things (see D&C 122:8). And He promised him that what he was called to endure would give him experience, work for his good, and ultimately lead to exaltation (see D&C 122:7).

What does that mean for us? You are probably on a much higher level, but frankly, I'm not always that humble or receptive when I hear my challenges are good for me or that things will work out eventually, especially when I'm caught in circumstances that seem beyond my ability to cope. What I prefer is a pat on the back for a job well done and the assurance that I've already suffered enough. And in my impatience and shortsightedness, I would like to know how it will work out and when it will work out and maybe even how hard it's going to be before it works out.

How do we focus on the eternal nature of our worth and lives, especially during times of special concern when perspective seems harder to come by? My mother told me something that helped her long ago when a task seemed bigger than she was. At the end of an already challenging pregnancy, she experienced a long and difficult labor. When she reached a point it all seemed too much to take, she told herself she could do anything for one minute. And then she would. And then she would do it again. She used that method sixty little seconds at a time until labor ended and she held her little one in her arms. It's akin to eating the proverbial elephant one small bite at a time.

Similarly, as we deal with the complexities of our mortal experience, taking a minute (or even a second) at a time might just be the best we can do. And even with our gospel perspective, we may tire of fighting exacting battles or facing our particular hardships, especially if they are long-term. While it's true that things will work out eventually, it's also true that some troubles may not be resolved for some time or possibly a lifetime.

I have come to know there are no easy answers or magic formulas for getting through those painful, soul-stretching experiences that come part and parcel with mortality. It's about taking a step at a time as we live and learn and make the very best decisions we can in our circumstances. When we are in those moments, we keep breathing, keep trying, and keep hoping for brighter days ahead, knowing the decisions we make and the disappointments we face are always seen more clearly when viewed through the lens of eternity.

As I previously mentioned, I used to naïvely believe that if I chose wisely enough and lived as well as I could, things would pretty much go the way I wanted them to. Maybe I'm not alone. For a while it came as a surprise to me when life didn't quite work out the way I expected. Experience is a great teacher, and I've learned through the years that I'm not in charge of everything I'd like to be. It's not as easy for me to accept as it is to say, but I try to remind myself that God knows what I can become, which sometimes means being uncomfortable in the proving process. Consider an enlightening analogy that invites us to examine the simple construction we might choose for ourselves as opposed to the more elaborate renovations of our Maker, who is building us. It's a lesson in perspective.

> Imagine yourself as a living house. God comes in to rebuild that house. At first, perhaps, you can understand what He is doing. He is getting the drains right and stopping the leaks in the roof and so on: you knew that those jobs needed doing and

so you are not surprised. But presently he starts knocking the house about in a way that hurts abominably and does not seem to make sense. What on earth is He up to? The explanation is that He is building quite a different house from the one you thought of—throwing out a new wing here, putting on an extra floor there, running up towers, making courtyards. You thought you were going to be made into a decent little cottage: but He is building a palace.[34]

My daughter Chelsey had a house-building experience right out of college as she embarked on a career as a graphic designer. A semester before graduation, she landed an internship that turned into a terrific job she had barely dared hope for as she made her way through school. As she worked those first few months, she was protective of her designs. She told me she often folded herself over her project so no one else could see while she was creating. As a junior designer, there was a catch. Before passing the finished product on to the client, she had to show it to her boss.

It's not surprising that those critiques were not her favorite part of the job. She'd put her heart and soul into her art, and it was uncomfortable having it viewed critically. It would have been much easier on her self-esteem if her boss had proclaimed the work perfect and given her the go-ahead without any recommendations, but that typically wasn't the case. He was kind, but as he went over her designs, he offered suggestions for improvement. Chelsey would take those suggestions and make the necessary changes. It didn't take long for her to realize that her boss, a respected and more experienced designer, had never failed to give her good advice. They built a relationship of trust, and she came to know that his constructive, instructive recommendations improved her initial efforts every single time.

Our Heavenly Father, the grand designer of the universe, is more experienced than we are. He knows the end from the beginning. With our own limited view, we usually don't have all the facts. If it were our choice alone, our lives would probably never include the adversity, disappointments, or even assignments and callings that make us stretch and grow in ways we didn't know we could. It is, however, those types of growing experiences that often provide the insights and understanding we wouldn't gain in any other way. Because God's ways are not our ways (see Isa. 55:8), in an expression of faith, we acquiesce that He knows what's better for us than we know ourselves.

34 C. S. Lewis, *Mere Christianity*, copyright © C. S. Lewis Pte. Ltd. 1942, 1943, 1944, 1952. Extract reprinted by permission.

If we allow them to work in us, His divine tutoring and uncomfortable or even painful adjustments make a positive difference in what we are making of ourselves for Him.

Perspective brings understanding and meaning to the decisions and experiences that fill each and every day. Whether it's a situation we're in, a trial we face, or a decision we need to make, perspective, especially eternal perspective, allows us to see things more the way God does in beautiful breadth and clarity. As Elder Neal A. Maxwell said, "*It is very important that we not assume the perspective of mortality in making the decisions that bear on eternity! We need the perspectives of the gospel to make decisions in the context of eternity.*"[35]

While we wouldn't choose to have trials or times of trouble, it's our experiences that make us what we are and help us as we strive to be the person our Heavenly Father knows we can become. I learned something in Primary from sweet Aspen when she shared her perspective. She said, "Even if bad things happen and things are hard, it's all part of our Heavenly Father's plan for us."[36] Though ten-year-old Aspen hasn't experienced some of the adversity and heartaches of adulthood, she has already been through some hard things in her young life. It was her childlike faith that allowed her to share her testimony of trials in such simple terms that made it sound so easy to accept them. Though our challenges aren't easily navigated, I know the insight Aspen shared with us is true. What we experience here as part of God's plan can mold and shape us into women of unshakable faith and courage and prepare us for all that our Father has.

I don't know all the reasons for the tests of life, but I am certain that the suffering we experience here isn't because our Heavenly Father doesn't love us, has forgotten us, or wants us to fail. When explaining the reason for our struggles, Elder Neal A. Maxwell offered his apostolic perspective: "Trials and tribulations tend to squeeze the artificiality out of us, leaving the essence of what we *really* are and clarifying what we *really* yearn for."[37]

He also offered the following clarification for those, like me, who wish for a life free of troubles: "A few individuals may appear to have no trial at all, which, if it were so, would be a trial in itself. Indeed, if our souls had rings, as do trees, to measure the years of greatest personal growth, the wide

---

35 Neal A. Maxwell, "But for a Small Moment" (Brigham Young University devotional, Sept. 1, 1974); speeches.byu.edu.

36 Personal notes in possession of the author.

37 Neal A. Maxwell, *Things as They Really Are* (Salt Lake City: Deseret Book Company, 1978), 89. Used with permission.

rings would likely reflect the years of greatest moisture—but from tears, not rainfall."[38]

Henry Wadsworth Longfellow also penned some poignant lines about rain:

> Be still, sad heart! and cease repining;
> Behind the clouds is the sun still shining;
> Thy fate is the common fate of all,
> Into each life some rain must fall.[39]

As father Lehi told Jacob, his firstborn in the wilderness, there is a reason for opposition in all things (see 2 Ne. 2:11). Adversity and trials humble us. Humility is a precursor to growth. We grow as we learn from our mistakes and triumph over trials that are essential to our learning process. Our Heavenly Father uses our experiences to make of us something we can't always see in ourselves, to prepare us to reign in His eternal courts above.

When we wonder about the grand design for our own lives, accepting His divine tutoring and loving instruction will improve our efforts every single time. Further, it is adopting the gospel viewpoint that encourages and enables us to move forward through all types of circumstances. While practicing perspective doesn't automatically erase the sting of disappointment, it can make a difference in how we deal with difficulties. Trying to see the big picture and holding fast to our faith in God's perspective helps us look beyond the fine print, beyond the moment, to catch a glimpse of who we really are.

---

38 Neal A. Maxwell, "Thanks Be to God," *Ensign*, Jul. 1982, 54.
39 Henry Wadsworth Longfellow, "The Rainy Day," *The Complete Poetical Works of Henry Wadsworth Longfellow*, Cambridge Edition, (Boston and New York: Houghton, Mifflin and Company, 1893), 16.

Chapter Eight
Heavenly Grandstands

Her self-esteem cannot be based on physical features, possession or lack of a particular talent, or comparative quantities of anything. Her self-esteem is earned by individual righteousness and a close relationship with God.[40] —Russell M. Nelson

DID YOU EVER HEAR THE words "Remember who you are" as you walked out the door on a date or to some other type of social activity in your youth? Though the familiar four-word phrase has been passed from parent to child countless times through the years, it isn't just words. It's an abbreviated way of saying, "Remember us. Remember where you came from and where you are going. Remember that we love you and want you to come home." The words echo a hope in every parent's heart that their son or daughter will let the knowledge of who they are, what they have been taught, and who they represent inspire their decisions while they are briefly separated from Mom or Dad's direct influence.

We can't remember what happened in our heavenly home as we prepared for our journey on earth, but it wouldn't be much of a stretch to imagine that our Heavenly Father hoped we understood some of the same things as we left His presence. Even though we have forgotten our life in that premortal realm, there is a glimmer—a flicker of recognition we brought with us—of who we are and who we have always been.

It's not a slight thing to understand we are children of God, but knowing isn't enough. Just as the four-word phrase suggests, we must remember who we are, wherever we are, in whatever we do. And as we remember, we let it make a difference in our decisions and our everyday interactions, which ultimately reflects in the way we feel about ourselves. Perhaps we focus more of our attention on sending that message to the rising generation, and rightly so. It is a difficult thing growing up in a challenging world, especially when trying to fit in. But crucibles

40 Russell M. Nelson, "Woman—Of Infinite Worth," *Ensign*, Nov. 1989, 20.

of confidence don't simply pass because we've left our formative years behind. As women—teachers, leaders, and examples—it's also vital that we embrace our divine heritage and reinforce it in our own lives as well.

Our Heavenly Father has made it clear in scripture and through the words of His servants that we matter to Him more than anything else. Since that sentiment doesn't serve Satan's selfish purposes, he tries to convince us that we are insignificant and small. Through both subtle means and overt actions, he works to persuade us that our value is based on physical qualities, personal property, people we know, worldly honors, successes, and countless other lies. He promotes these ideas in an effort to confuse us and undermine our feelings of worth in order to stunt our growth and limit our progress and power. It's part of his attempt to prevent us from living as purposefully and confidently as we can. He applauds only superficial achievements because he doesn't want us to find lasting happiness or to succeed in a meaningful, eternal way.

Satan knows who we are, and he has from the beginning. He was there with us. With his own growth stunted, he delights in interfering with our connection to our Heavenly Father because he knows how crucial it is. While the adversary doesn't have the power to change who we are, he doesn't stop trying. He takes great pleasure in feeding our doubts and fueling our insecurities in the hope of distancing us from God and the atoning power of our Savior, Jesus Christ. Misery loves company, and the adversary wants us to be miserable like he is. Elder Jörg Klebingat said, "Whenever the adversary cannot persuade imperfect yet striving Saints such as you to abandon your belief in a personal and loving God, he employs a vicious campaign to put as much distance as possible between you and God. . . . [H]e will seek access to your heart to tell you lies—lies that Heavenly Father is disappointed in you, that the Atonement is beyond your reach, that there is no point in even trying, that everyone else is better than you, that you are unworthy, and a thousand variations of that same evil theme."[41]

One of the many tools we have to combat his underhanded efforts is staying close to our Heavenly Father and basing our worth on His love. The things we already know about that relationship aren't just a list to keep us too busy or to add to our guilt when we don't do them as well as we'd like. Rather, the principles and practices of the gospel help us remain firm and immovable in our faith and in our connection to Him. We repent often and listen to His Spirit and then act on the promptings we receive. We regularly attend our church meetings to gain understanding and inspiration and to rededicate ourselves to His work. We take the sacrament, renew sacred baptismal covenants, and feel the newness

---

41 Jörg Klebingat, "Approaching the Throne of God with Confidence," *Ensign*, Nov. 2014, 34.

of life that comes from being clean again. We delight in the Sabbath day and the strength it gives us to move forward with faith into another week. We read the scriptures for understanding and personal direction. We communicate with Him through prayer and then follow as He directs. We attend the temple. We confide in Him. We share our joys and victories, our hopes and heartaches, our problems, insecurities, and pain. We offer gratitude for His help, and we call upon Him whenever we are in need. As we do so and even as we are lacking, He will answer and remind us of His love.

When you wonder if God loves you or is aware of you, ask Him yourself. Don't listen for one minute to the messages coming from that someone else who cares only about himself.

Many years ago, I called out silently when I felt I was falling short. I was cleaning the bathroom, which might seem like a funny place for personal revelation, unless you are in high demand in your home like women are. The bathroom is my favorite place for inspiration, and it's not because of the acoustics. I often receive answers when I'm cleaning, showering, or washing my hair, and I've figured out why. When my children were younger, they followed me everywhere. The one exception was the bathroom, especially when I was cleaning, most likely because they were afraid I might put them to work. One day I was alone on my knees, scrubbing the floor and silently reviewing some of the things that were troubling me. (Reviewing is probably too nice a word for what I was doing. I was actually giving myself a good mental beating.) I felt like I wasn't doing well with my responsibilities, that I was running as fast as I could but wasn't anywhere close to keeping up. As a result, I wondered if I was letting my Heavenly Father down. In a little throw-in-the-towel-type moment, I sighed and said to myself, *I'm doing the best I can.* A gentle reply came swiftly and silently, yet spoke directly to my heart. *I know you are, and I love you.* I can't begin to explain how that felt for me then, and I can't enumerate the times I've gone back to that sweet assurance of God's love for me when I doubt myself.

The Old Testament tells of the prophet Elisha's awareness that God was there while he was encircled about by Syrians, who were not coming for Sunday brunch, by the way. When surrounded by this formidable foe, his servant saw myriad horses and chariots and was understandably afraid. Elisha answered his questioning brother with faith.

> Fear not: for they that be with us are more than they that be with them.
>
> And Elisha prayed, and said, Lord, I pray thee, open his eyes, that he may see. And the Lord opened the eyes of the young man; and he saw: and, behold, the mountain was full of horses and chariots of fire round about Elisha. (2 Kgs. 6:16–17)

Just as with Elisha of old, there is heavenly help available to us too, whenever, wherever we need it, even if we don't always see or recognize it right away. Elder Jeffrey R. Holland reminds us, "In the gospel of Jesus Christ you have help from both sides of the veil."[42]

For myself, in my weakness, I've had occasion to wonder if my Father in Heaven is there for me, especially in the midst of trouble or concern. On the other side of trouble, with clearer perspective, I can always see His influential hand moving in my life. And I have often been humbled and amazed by the realization of what He has done.

For many years, I worked as a stay-at-home mom. When my husband, the primary breadwinner in our family, was out of work for an extended period, I secured three jobs to help supplement our income. With no specific training and limited education beyond high school, I took the work I could find. In doing so, I found myself working into the wee hours of the morning just to keep up. I was getting very little sleep—often only a few hours a day—and I was struggling in many ways. During a visit, a wise and caring visiting teacher commented that I must have been receiving heavenly help to keep it all going. Right at that moment, I was exhausted and was actually wondering where that help was. In my view, the resolution was for my husband to find a job immediately, not for me to be able to keep up with the numerous jobs I had. I later learned I was wrong, which is an all-too-frequent occurrence, I'm afraid. My Heavenly Father had blessed me immensely throughout that time; it took some time and distance from the situation, but I know that now in looking back. I can see Him carrying me through. He was the reason I made it in one piece. I didn't recognize it at first because of some misplaced resentment, but that didn't mean He wasn't there with me every step of the way.

I learned another lesson about His help one summer night while watching my son Mason play baseball. His team was participating in a weekend tournament. The boys had won a lot of games and landed in the finals. It was early evening when the two opposing teams took the field. Players and spectators alike were either hungry, sunburned, exhausted, or a delightful combination of the three. Still, it was thrilling. All the hard work and practice that had gone into that moment had finally paid off.

I remember like it was yesterday sitting on the old wooden bleachers at the ballpark in beautiful Providence, Utah. Dusk had settled, and the summer air was heavy and hot. The game was played under the lights, like a giant stage, players illuminated by spotlight.

---

42 Jeffrey R. Holland, "For Times of Trouble" (Brigham Young University devotional, Mar. 18, 1980); speeches.byu.edu.

Time stood still for me a few minutes into the game. I can't recall if the particular play on the field was a monster hit, a remarkable catch, or something else. Whatever it was, it evoked a huge reaction from the crowd and played out for me as if in slow motion. I was intensely aware of the noise from the crowd. I was thrilled that the boys had an entire grandstand cheering like crazy for them. In that moment, I also tried to remember the last time anyone had cheered like that for me. It had happened in my youth, but lately no one was clapping when I found the bottom of the hamper. I never got a high five for emptying the dishwasher or dusting underneath the knick-knacks rather than around them. And then a remembrance of something President Ezra Taft Benson said many years ago filled my mind and heart: "The heavenly grandstands are cheering you on."[43] My Heavenly Father gently let me know that in all His grand and glorious responsibilities, amid all that was going on in the world and amid the more pressing needs of those who were truly suffering, He was aware of me, aware of where I was, aware of what I was feeling.

After years and years of summer baseball games and double-header Saturdays, I've learned that no matter how cliché it sounds, baseball *is* like life in so many ways. Every day we step up to the plate. Sometimes we make contact with the ball. Sometimes we strike out. Sometimes we're in a slump that's difficult to overcome. If we're lucky, we hit a home run now and then. We catch, we juggle, we drop the ball. Some days and moments we win, and other times we feel like we come up short no matter what we do or how hard we try. Remember, wherever we are in the game, whatever we do, however we feel, we have help from the other side of the veil. We have heavenly grandstands cheering us on. Through all that happens during the ins and outs of our lives, our Heavenly Father remembers us, and He wants us to remember Him. He also wants us to know He is there, ever loving us, pulling for us, cheering us on, and longing for us to come home.

---

43 Ezra Taft Benson, "In His Steps" (Brigham Young University devotional, Mar. 4, 1979); speeches.byu.edu.

Chapter Nine
By Invitation Only

Feelings of worth come when a woman follows the example of the Master.[44]
—Russell M. Nelson

NOT ONLY DID THE SAVIOR suffer for our sins and die for us centuries ago, but He lives and continues His work for us today. We previously addressed that His sacrifice in our behalf was the most generous act of all time and is awe-inspiring to think of in terms of our personal worth. Knowing and believing in what He did for us has a marvelous impact on how we feel about and view ourselves, but an enduring relationship with Him is the answer to the self-doubt, insecurity, and loneliness we all feel from time to time. As we look to Him, His steady influence lifts us and fills us with light and confidence. No matter where we are, He is ready for us, ever inviting us to come unto Him.

In the course of a lifetime, we are going to receive a lot of invitations. They come in all shapes, sizes, and styles. Some are casual, fun, and festive. Others are fancy and formal. In this Internet era, they are often delivered via email, text, or another type of social media. While many are extended online, still others are presented in person or stamped and sent through the mail. There are invitations we seek and welcome and others we probably don't. They bid our attendance at birthday parties, wedding receptions, baby showers, and countless other special occasions.

Allow me to share the tale of two invitations. One was more recent and printed carefully by the hand of a child on the back of a note about something else. *Dear Wendy,* it began. *Please come to my house and watch our show. Love, the Show People.* The *Show People* were three of my young neighborhood friends who had delivered the invitation and run. Apparently, they had been working for a while on an original play about princesses. It was an exclusive

---

44 Russell M. Nelson, "Woman—Of Infinite Worth," *Ensign*, Nov. 1989, 20.

engagement, and I was fortunate enough to be invited. Wild horses couldn't have kept me away.

Having rescheduled the performance many times due to unforeseen circumstances like dinner and soccer practice and chores, just before the real curtain, those adorable little actors came for me. They chatted happily as they escorted me to the comfortable theater seating, which was actually a couch in the basement of one of their homes. I was thrilled to be there, and they seemed excited I'd come. The only other audience member was one of the girl's mothers. When the play commenced, the girls were sweet and silly as they acted on their make-believe stage the scenes they had previously rehearsed. The production was also sprinkled with plenty of hilarious impromptu lines I could tell by the others' reactions were departures from their script. (I would have expected nothing less from my five-year-old friends.) It was one of the most entertaining thirty minutes I'd spent in some time and one of the favorite invitations I've ever received.

The second was a bunch of invitations I extended that stand in contrast to that delightful event. (Though the experience is uncomfortable, bear with me—I share it only to illustrate a point. Whenever I think about it now, I remind myself that we must know the bitter to appreciate the sweet.) Many years ago, a dear friend of mine had recently started selling a popular product through home parties and asked me to host one for her. I was immediately hesitant and suddenly insecure because I was afraid no one would come. I told her as much. I didn't want to waste her time, and truthfully, I was just as concerned about what it meant for my self-esteem if no one showed. Still, she was always good to me, and I wanted to help. After some coaxing, I finally agreed.

We picked a night and time that worked for both of us, and I sent invitations to several friends and neighbors. I cleaned my little apartment and made a treat. My friend arrived early to set up her display. After the appointed hour, we waited. Then we waited and waited some more. There were no doorbells ringing or knocks on the door. Eventually it became glaringly clear that no one was coming, just as I had first feared. All was not lost, because we had a nice visit. We talked for a while before she gathered her things. She was so kind about it, especially considering it was a huge waste of time for her.

As I recall, the doorbell rang just before she left. One guest, another good friend, stood on my doorstep. I was grateful she'd come, but by that time it didn't make much difference in how I felt. The personal fallout from that experience prompted some temporary feelings of exclusion and isolation, especially since I'd been to many home parties before, and I was pretty sure mine was the only one since the beginning of time with no guests. Years have passed since then.

I'm mostly over any measurable negative feelings that failed attempt at a party caused for me back then. I say mostly because, if I'm being honest, I've never thrown another one. I wouldn't dare tempt fate.

I think we are very aware and sensitive to the challenges of loneliness in adolescence that are associated with being left out. But even as adults, inclusion or exclusion often factors into the way we feel about ourselves. Young, old, or in-between, there will forever be groups that get together without us when we'd like to be involved, parties and events that go on in our absence, and gatherings we do attend but still feel left out of, for whatever reason. But even when these experiences are painful or uncomfortable or perhaps even embarrassing, they have no bearing on who we are or how much we matter.

The Savior extends an invitation to each of us without regard to popularity, social status, or social standing. It is the most important invitation we will ever receive and makes all the rest seem insignificant in the eternal scheme of things. In simple words recorded in ancient text, Jesus Christ beckons us to come unto Him, to follow Him (see Matt. 11:28 and D&C 88:63). He also gently entreats us, "Learn of me, and listen to my words; walk in the meekness of my Spirit, and you shall have peace in me" (D&C 19:23). He calls to those who labor and are laden with care (see Matt. 11:28). He calls to the meek and poor in spirit (see Matt. 5:3, 5). His message of inclusion echoes to the ends of the earth, and His offer of peace extends to all who heed His call. Elder Jeffrey R. Holland shared this comforting thought: "Whoever we are and whatever our problems, his response is always the same, forever: 'Come unto me.'"[45]

Though the Savior suffered for our sins, the Atonement isn't only for when we sin or fall short. Whatever our situation, He knows how we feel. As we turn to Him, He dispels the pain of loneliness and the hurts and the slights and the struggles in our lives. He understands exactly and completely. He also understands rejection in a way no one else can. Of the Savior, Isaiah said, "He is despised and rejected of men; a man of sorrows, and acquainted with grief: and we hid as it were our faces from him; he was despised, and we esteemed him not" (Isa. 53:3).

Near the end of His life, when love and support were needed more than ever, Jesus was alone in the Garden of Gethsemane. He didn't start out that way, having traveled there with some of His most beloved Apostles. You'll recall that He invited them to pray with Him, to stay with Him in this hour of great agony. As He departed from them to take upon Himself all the sins and pain and loneliness mankind would ever experience, they slept. In this most significant

---

45 Jeffrey R. Holland, "Come unto Me" (Brigham Young University devotional, Mar. 2, 1997); speeches.byu.edu.

experience of His life, three times He asked them to watch and pray; three times He returned to find them sleeping.

Later, He was betrayed and denied by friends and also falsely accused. He was sent to His Crucifixion as the crowd chose to end His innocent life over another who had broken the law. He was mocked, beaten, and spat upon. His anguish at His Crucifixion, where he cried out in agony of total aloneness, is well beyond our mortal comprehension. Because of His experience in those and other lonely moments, Jesus Christ is uniquely qualified to succor us in our own.

When we are broken and afraid, He helps us believe in ourselves. In our hour of need, He is not sleeping but is there. Though perfect, He shows us how we can overcome weakness and sin. As our Elder Brother, He desires to lift us up and help us home. Jesus said, "My grace is sufficient for thee: for my strength is made perfect in weakness" (2 Cor. 12:9). His grace makes us whole, transforms us, strengthens us, and helps us live better lives.

I've always thought of His grace as something that's applied at the judgment seat of God after everything is said and done and we're reaping our eternal reward. Brother Brad Wilcox explained a different and enlightening perspective. He said, "Grace is not a booster engine that kicks in once our fuel supply is exhausted. Rather, it is our constant energy source. It is not the light at the end of the tunnel but the light that moves us through the tunnel. Grace is not achieved somewhere down the road. It is received right here and right now."[46]

What a relief it is to accept our Savior's invitation, to count on His grace when we need it most, even in this very moment. In addition, we can rely on His strength when we are lacking our own. As the Apostle Paul said, we can do all things through Christ, who strengthens us (see Phil. 4:13).

Many years ago, I heard of a sister in a nearby community who was struggling with numerous health problems. She was also facing financial setbacks and was the sole caretaker of children with disabilities. In an effort to keep going through all of her heartache and disappointment, she placed a picture of the Savior in every room of her home. As she dealt with the trials in her life and as she moved through her home taking care of her various responsibilities, she focused on a picture of the Savior and relied on Him as she committed to carry the weight of her load with His help.

Just like this good sister, we find strength in our Savior to fight our battles, whatever they are. He gives us confidence and courage to stand by our

46 Brad Wilcox, "His Grace Is Sufficient" (Brigham Young University devotional, July 12, 2011); speeches.byu.edu.

convictions. In addition, He has promised His companionship when we feel alone. Through Him we have the surety that even in times of isolation, we are never truly alone. He offers His understanding and compassion. He points us toward our divine potential and makes of our lives something we never could without His guiding hand. We don't have to do anything to qualify for His love, but as we accept His invitation and draw close to Him, we access His unequaled power in our lives.

In the book of Matthew, chapter 22, we read an important parable in which the Savior likened the kingdom of heaven to a certain king who planned a wedding celebration for his son. At the appointed hour, the king sent his servants to issue a royal reminder to his invited guests. After no one showed up to this event of all events (the king wasn't selling Tupperware), he again dispatched his servants to bid attendance and declare that everything was ready—a feast and all that a royal wedding entailed. It made no difference. Rather than feeling it was an honor to be included, the prospective guests made light of the invitation as they went about their business. Even worse than that, a remnant of them killed the servants who had delivered the request. (Talk about shooting the messenger.)

Since one might imagine some ramifications in rejecting a personal invitation from a king, who wouldn't make every effort to attend a royal wedding, especially if there was going to be food? It was not a last-minute request, and it seems the guests had plenty of time to prepare. The scriptures don't detail the reasons the invitees chose not to attend, so we can only guess about their excuses. Maybe they'd attended one too many weddings that week. Maybe some had misplaced their invitations or had a scheduling conflict because they hadn't saved the date on their calendar or iPhone. Maybe they forgot to buy a gift. Whatever the reason, the entire bunch rejected the royal invitation, leaving the king to scramble and fill the hall with replacements from the streets and highways.

There are many lessons to be learned from the parable. For our purposes, we'll focus on those who were invited but chose not to come even after considerable reminders. Since I'm guilty of forgetting a wedding or two in my life, even important ones, I get it. But this was not your run-of-the-mill affair. The invitation is most significant when we consider who it came from and whom the king and his son, the groom, represent. Unlike weddings we go to, attendance at this wedding was not as much a request as it was a command. The guests were expected to be there, especially considering the second chance they had to get their collective acts together and attend.

One of the applications of the parable and a key for us today lies in accepting the King's invitation, not just so we can be ready to greet the Bridegroom when He comes again, but so we can have His love and sustaining power with us today and always. Our relationship with the Savior, unlike attendance at a wedding, is not a one-time event. It involves our conscientious attention and preparation on an everyday basis. It's not some destination we arrive at, check off our list, and for which we throw the invitation away. We value it and keep it close and accept it every day of our lives.

It's not uncommon for many types of invitations to include the fancy little French postscript, *RSVP*. I'm not sure exactly how to say it, but we all know what it means. A reply in the affirmative often means bringing something to the party—a birthday gift, a wedding present, etcetera. Accepting the Savior's invitation doesn't require fancy words or beautifully wrapped packages. He asks for our humble hearts and willing hands. The peace and protection He offers are incredible blessings in an increasingly turbulent world. We respond to His invitation by learning of Him, worshiping Him, repenting of our sins, and doing our best to emulate the qualities He exemplifies. We keep the commandments not to repay Him for all He has done, because we never could, but because we love Him, want to be like Him, and desire to have Him near us always. When we have taken His name upon us and felt to sing the song of His redeeming love (see Alma 5:26), we are changed forever. We can never be the same again! As we let His love influence and envelope us, we are better able to see ourselves the way He does.

I once read the story of a woman who received an invitation to a different wedding feast than the one described in Matthew. This one came from an old friend. The author mentioned she was hesitant to accept it at first because she knew she would be going alone and was afraid she'd feel out of place. In the end, she decided she simply couldn't turn down the request. She arrived just before the wedding dinner began and quickly spotted an empty seat. She made her way to the table and asked if the place was taken. She was taken aback when a woman at the table asked her if she was supposed to be there.

The wedding guest responded politely that she was a friend of the groom. After some uncomfortable moments, she noticed him seated at the front of the hall with his bride. He was the only one in the room she recognized. When he saw her too, he stood and placed his hand over his heart—a gesture to let her know how much it meant to him that she was there. The guest was filled with relief. No matter what anyone else thought, the groom let her know she belonged. She shared these touching thoughts: "Obedience is the only requirement for accepting an invitation from Jesus Christ to rejoice with Him, to have a place at His feast. And that feast is one at which guests need never feel insecure because they *do* belong. Although I am yet far from perfect in my obedience, I hope one day to qualify to meet the Bridegroom and with hand over heart—a heart submitted to His will—say, 'I'm so happy to be here.'"[47]

Our Savior lovingly calls to us and encourages us. It is the adversary who whispers messages of inadequacy to our hearts and minds. Satan enjoys it when we doubt ourselves and our eternal standing with our Heavenly Father and Jesus Christ. He hopes to convince us that we aren't good enough to accept the Savior's invitation or that we aren't worthy of a relationship with Him or that all is lost because we aren't perfect like we should be. He would have us believe that how we live doesn't matter, that Jesus Christ isn't aware of us, doesn't care what we do, or worse, that He simply doesn't exist. But the Savior lives! And He has shown how He cares for us with every act of love and selflessness He has offered us.

In the familiar scene from the New Testament, Jesus met with His disciples in an upper room where they shared a last supper. After He tenderly washed their feet and dismissed the one who would later betray Him, He taught those who remained. It is evident in the verses there that as our Savior faced the end of His life and mortal ministry, He was most concerned for those He would leave behind. He promised He would not leave them comfortless but would come unto them (see John 14:16–18). He will come to us too. Elder Jeffrey R. Holland explained, "Because he must ultimately tread this winepress of redemption unaided, can he endure the darkest moment of them all, the shock of the greatest pain? This comes not with thorns and with nails, but with the terror of feeling utterly alone: . . . Can he bear all of our sins *and* our fear and loneliness too? He did and he does and he will."[48]

We mustn't forget that not only is Jesus Christ our Savior, but He is also our loving friend. He possesses all the qualities of a dear friend, like compassion, dependability, loyalty, and unconditional love, without any of the mortal shortcomings. Only He can perfectly understand. He will support us in our joys and successes and carry us through hardship and trial. He will succor us in our infirmities, sorrows, and self-doubts. We can always rely on Him. When we allow His love in our lives, it will reflect in our eyes as we carry it with us in everything we do. That confidence frees us to worry less about what matters in the world and more about what matters most.

Social gatherings will come and go. Parties and get-togethers will continue to happen with or without us. It's always nice to be included, but our worth is not counted in parties we attend or in the number of friends and admirers we have. In the eternal scheme of things, when all is said and done, the

---

47 Melissa Merrill, "A Seat at the Bridegroom's Feast," *Ensign*, Feb. 2011, 80.
48 Jeffrey R. Holland, "He Loved Them unto the End," *Ensign*, Nov. 1989, 25.

invitations we receive won't matter very much as long as we continually accept the invitation that comes from our Savior, Jesus Christ.

Chapter Ten
Can You Hear Me Now?

It is the Spirit who reveals to us our identity—which isn't just who we are but who we have always been. And when we know, our lives take on a sense of purpose so stunning that we can never be the same again.[49] —Sheri L. Dew

SOME OF THE MESSAGES WE hear frequently in the world today are very different from the affirmations of the still small voice of the Spirit. While those other voices are often confusing, His messages to us are clear. He will remind us of who we are and why we matter so much. He will inform us of and inspire us to fulfill our own personal mission. His quiet communications directly contradict what Satan throws in our faces every single day. His light fills our souls and helps chase the dark clouds of discouragement and self-doubt away.

We know the Holy Ghost comforts us, warns us of danger, and helps us choose between right and wrong. He also enlightens our minds and speaks truth to us about ourselves and our everlasting connection to our heavenly home. It is through the Holy Ghost's voice that our Father in Heaven conveys the things He wants us to know, allowing for the personal direction that enables us to hold strong to our convictions and stand against the destructive messages swirling about us.

Sister Sheri Dew shared this perspective: "The adversary *delights* in separating us, the sisters of this Church, from the Spirit. Because he knows how vital our influence and our presence is in the latter-day kingdom of God."[50] Having the Spirit with us is essential as we seek a steady sense of worth. He provides the inspiration to build our lives and understand our vital role in building God's kingdom on earth.

---

49 Sheri L. Dew, "Knowing Who You Are—and Who You Have Always Been" (Brigham Young University Women's Conference, May 4, 2001); womensconference.byu.edu.
50 Sheri L. Dew, "We Are Not Alone," *Ensign*, Nov. 1998, 96.

You might be familiar with a cell phone commercial that depicts all sorts of circumstances and settings that could make reception difficult. It's amusing to see the caller in a cornfield, a rain storm, a bowling alley, or on a bus, all while asking the question, "Can you hear me now?" The premise is that the provider offers superior service and boasts that even with interference, good reception is still possible, which is exactly how the Spirit works in our lives.

It brings to mind a verse in Alma that says in part, "Can you feel so now?" (Alma 5:26). Alma was asking about the state of our conversion, but we could ask ourselves the same question in regard to the Holy Ghost, especially as we consider messages from Him; it's so much more about feeling than hearing. If we've felt the Spirit once, can we feel His presence still? A familiar scripture asks if we have ears to hear (see Matt. 11:15), but more often than not, we usually hear the voice of the Spirit with our hearts. When we have felt His presence and experienced the peace that accompanies these special communications, we want to do whatever we can to feel His influence now and always. Since we never want to lose His guidance in our lives, we must stand where He can reach us physically and figuratively.

Years ago, something that happened on a family weekend getaway to Park City, Utah, offered a parallel into how to better cultivate the influence of the Spirit in my life. As we began our journey, everyone piled into the car and we drove the short distance to the Kimball Junction exit. We made our way to a winding road that meandered past fields, a country church, and an old farmhouse. If you've been there, you know how lovely it is, nestled against the majestic Wasatch Mountain Range. We were all enjoying the warm day and breathtaking scenery when we noticed that the drivers of several cars ahead of us had pulled to the side of the road. Spectators had spilled out here and there along the shoulder with binoculars and cameras in hand, but initially we couldn't tell what they were spectating. Mostly out of curiosity, we also slowed down and pulled to the side of the road because we wanted to get in on the action, whatever it was.

Once we stopped, we quickly recognized the reason for all the fuss. Just off the road, fewer than sixty feet from our stopping point, an enormous moose grazed in a grassy field. He was spectacular with his giant antlers, knobby knees, and long, lean legs. As he munched on foliage, he seemed completely unaware of the gathering crowd. In order to see him better, we decided to get out of the car. What we didn't anticipate was that our enthusiastic children would exit the vehicle at roughly the same decibel level as a large marching band, tubas and drums and all. When they did, the moose noticed all of us and immediately moved on to greener (or at least quieter) pastures. Sadly, so did everyone else. While we probably should have issued an apology for the public disturbance, we quickly got back in the car, feeling a little sheepish that our rowdy bunch had ended the moment for everyone else. But at least we caught a quick glimpse of that magnificent moose.

On the surface, it might seem a little silly to compare how the whisperings of the Holy Ghost have anything to do with our moose sighting. But I've thought about it in that very context through the years and reached the conclusion that tucked in that experience are some hidden gems that point directly to cultivating the constancy of His companionship.

In that circumstance, if we hadn't been paying attention, especially with all that was going on in our car with three young children, we would have driven past the moose without even noticing he was there. While that might have been fortunate for everyone else, we would have missed the experience entirely. And even though we saw him for just a few fleeting moments, we were certainly glad we did.

It doesn't take living very long to realize that life comes at us fast, especially as adults. I sometimes feel like life as a grown-up is reminiscent of those old dodgeball games we used to play in gym—balls furiously flying everywhere! Though the game was fast-paced, being fast wasn't always the solution, unless one was leaping frantically away from a surprise attack. The better strategy was being attentive and perceptive by keeping an eye on the balls. It was always better and safer to see them coming than to get out of the way any way one could to avoid being pegged. The object was to dodge, duck, and evade all while keeping the other balls in play as well.

In like manner, the object in life is not to run just as fast as we can but rather to evade what the adversary throws our way through careful avoidance of things that could take us out of the game. The companionship of the Holy Ghost is that incomparable protection in our fast-paced lives. We simply cannot afford not to have His influence in all the big moments and everyday decisions. Since the messages of the Spirit are often as brief as they are quiet, we don't want to miss them because we aren't paying attention.

Another key element in our moose sighting was slowing down. It was the first thing we did after we saw the growing crowd at the side of the road. It certainly wasn't advisable to approach a soft shoulder driving the posted speed limit. Likewise, our many responsibilities often require us to move a hundred miles an hour just to keep up. That can be physically taxing as well as spiritually draining. When we're moving quickly, it's harder to filter out the static and tune in to the Spirit. Inspiration comes most often in quiet, contemplative moments. Slowing down and opening our hearts provides space for messages from the Spirit to reach us. Slowing down also allows us to take time for the fundamental actions that build the type of relationship that consistently keeps us in tune.

Finally, we came to a stop. The moose was right off the road, so we could have looked at him from our car windows at forty miles per hour if we preferred. However, we enjoyed a much better view when we pulled over and got out of the car. In life, when slowing down isn't enough, sometimes we need to stop, go to our knees, and ask for direction or affirmation.

I was touched by a story I read of a woman who had endured many years of infertility. Her heart was heavy, and her relationship with Heavenly Father and everyone around her had suffered. Several years into the struggle, she realized she was bitter because she believed her innumerable unanswered prayers for a child meant that she wasn't loved. One day that realization brought her again to her knees, where she had been so many times before. Perhaps we've all had similar feelings in our own set of difficult circumstances. Perhaps we've all wondered whether or not we are loved. In her prayer, she asked simply, "Do you love me?"[51] As soon as she uttered the words, she was overwhelmed with feelings of love, joy, and peace. Heavenly Father had heard her pleas and conveyed a personal message to her heart through the quiet whisperings of the Holy Spirit. The loving reinforcement made all the difference in her life as the bitterness fell away.

Conveying messages from our Father is one of the Spirit's important responsibilities. For us, there are some answers from the Spirit that come to our heart and mind that are best received on our knees. There are also times when we're seeking guidance that staying on our knees following prayer facilitates the answer because we are listening and quietly awaiting the reply.

In a nutshell, the real reason the moose ran away wasn't the fact that we'd stopped to see him. He already had several admirers at the side of the road and they hadn't bothered him a bit. In fact, he acted as if he had no clue they were there. The issue arose from our family's disruptive arrival. I'm confident the moose would have munched on foliage and continued to ignore the gathering crowd if we hadn't been so obvious and loud.

As I saw the experience unfold for our family, it was a situation I recognized well. There have been occasions in my life when I felt like the messages from the Spirit weren't getting through, not always because of physical noise, per se,

---

51 Tamara A. Ilich, "I Longed to Be a Mother," *Ensign*, Aug. 2000, 59.

but because of the commotion caused by my thoughts darting from one place to another or being so consumed with worry that I couldn't focus long enough to listen. Stress and worry will do that. Maybe you can relate. Someone once told me that women are like helicopters when it comes to how we think. We hover a bit and then dart to something else, and so on and so on, never resting in one place for very long. (She also said that men are more like giant cargo ships in the way they cruise in one direction and are often more singularly focused, but that is another topic entirely.)

That analogy hit home for me because I am a woman and my brain is exactly like a helicopter, especially during times of worry and concern. When inspiration has been hard to come by, I'm often reminded of the words to a favorite scripture that invites us to be still (see D&C 101:16). Many times, I've had to trust the entreating invitation and choose to be still—mentally, physically, and spiritually. What works for me is finding a quiet room in an effort to contain my unproductive thoughts and tuning in to the messages from the Spirit. Sometimes, in those moments when I need to set myself aside, I repeat the words of the above-referenced scripture about stillness or hum the hymn "Be Still, My Soul."[52] It has always worked, being still, though it doesn't always happen automatically or without some concerted effort on my part. The scripture alludes to a spiritual stillness, but I've found that literally holding still and seeking a secluded spot helps to facilitate the process of settling my heart and mind. It makes perfect sense that being still enables us to better hear the promptings of the still small voice.

All of this is not to say we will *only* be able to hear the Spirit if we are in quiet places. We won't always have that opportunity, and sometimes we're going to need inspiration on the run, among a crowd, or bustling through our busy lives. It's nice when we can set ourselves apart from all the noise and listen, but all is not lost if we can't. When we're in tune, we can train ourselves to hear His voice through the chaos.

Pardon another sports analogy, especially so close to the last, but my husband has often shared a valuable experience of a contentious basketball game that relates to the ability we can have to feel the Spirit's influence even through the din of life. The battle was between his high school team and a rival team in another small community. The gymnasium was always loud there, but it wasn't only the cheering of fans that raised the roof. There were also cowbells. Cowbells! In the final seconds of one tight game, a member of my husband's team was on the free-throw line shooting for some crucial points. In an effort

---

52   "Be Still, My Soul," *Hymns*, no. 124.

to distract the player shooting, the sound from the crowd in the bleachers went from a dull roar to deafening, cowbells only adding to the chaos. Amazingly, even in the din, my husband clearly heard his coach on the sidelines relaying last-second instructions to the team about what to do after the final foul shot.

What enabled his ability to hear his coach's voice with all the volume going on around him? He attributes it to the training. He and the other team members had spent invaluable practice time in a quiet gym listening to their coach. Because they had learned to recognize his voice, they could hear it as it cut through all the other, louder noises in that basketball arena.

In a similar way, we can train ourselves to hear the voice of the Spirit in quiet moments and also in the chaos that sometimes happens in our lives. It is the practice of listening to and acting on the messages we receive from Him that makes us better listeners. The more we listen, the easier it becomes to hear the Spirit speaking to us. Scripture tells us that His voice is still and small, but it whispers through and pierces all things (see D&C 85:6). We are able to filter out the noise around us and let His words pierce and penetrate our hearts and souls because of the stillness on the inside and also because we have come to recognize His voice.

It is a worthy goal and of paramount importance to always have His Spirit to be with us, as we are promised at baptism (see D&C 20:77). His companionship creates in us a serenity and lightness we can't obtain in any other way.

When I was little and my family would gather to watch television together, I would often pick a spot in the middle of the room and plop right down on the floor without paying any attention to whose view of the screen I was blocking. My mom would ask me to scoot a little to the left or right by gently reminding me that I made a better door than a window. As an adult, I often think about this question in a figurative way: How often do I still make a better door than a window?

We all want to be more like windows than doors when it comes to the Holy Ghost. Rather than blocking His light, we want it to stream through us, fill us, and reflect in our countenance. We do that by purifying our lives to receive that light. Like any other important relationship in our lives, the constant companionship of the Holy Ghost requires attention and tender care. There is nothing we don't already know about our part in that relationship-building effort. What we review in church each week, like regularly attending church and the temple, partaking of the sacrament, studying the scriptures, praying frequently, having faith, practicing repentance, having love in our hearts, being kind, and showing charity, are the building blocks of that very special association. The development of these habits and attributes makes us more inclined to receive spiritual promptings. And consistently acting upon the promptings from the Holy Ghost enables us to better interpret His instructions while making us more likely to receive continued promptings.

Scripture describes the companionship of the Holy Ghost as an "unspeakable gift" (see D&C 121:26). Indescribable, inexpressible, remarkable, unimaginable, and many other superlatives apply. Whatever word we use to describe this amazing blessing, how we feel in His companionship is worth whatever it takes to have Him with us always.

One of the most memorable experiences of my youth came from practicing a song for an upcoming sacrament meeting presentation with the rest of the Primary. That year we had learned the lovely, "Teach Me to Walk in the Light." It is still one of my favorites, perhaps because of this experience. We sang the song as a group, but as we reached the closing line, "Teach me, teach me to walk in the light,"[53] some of the older children broke into parts. Unbeknownst to the rest of us, the chorister had been working with some of the senior Primary classes and had taught them a simple harmony. It was unexpected and made quite an impression on me. I had heard the song many times before, but never like that. It was thrilling. I remember feeling like someone had turned a light on. I can't adequately describe how it touched my young heart, but I remember.

Being in tune with the Holy Ghost is certainly not a new concept. Nothing can compare to the brightness and harmony we feel when we have the Spirit with us. It's like letting the light flood a darkened room. As we meet tests and challenges, make important decisions, and find our way with meaning and purpose in a difficult world, we simply cannot afford to be without His companionship. When we're in that place of peace that accompanies the influence of the Spirit, we feel spiritually healthy, physically stronger, more capable, and more confident, which reflects in the way we feel about ourselves and everything else as well. What else does the companionship of the Holy Ghost do for us? Sister Sheri Dew said, "No amount of time in front of the mirror will make you as attractive as having the Holy Ghost with you."[54] And Sister Linda K. Burton said, "The Holy Ghost can do for us physically, spiritually, emotionally, mentally, and intellectually what no man-made remedy can begin to duplicate."[55]

53 "Teach Me to Walk in the Light," *Children's Songbook*, 177.

54 Sheri L. Dew, "It Is Not Good for Man or Woman to Be Alone," *Ensign*, Nov. 2001, 13.

55 Linda K. Burton, "Tuning Our Hearts to the Voice of the Spirit" (CES Devotional for Young Adults, Brigham Young University–Idaho, Mar. 2, 2014); lds.org/broadcasts.

The Holy Spirit gives us strength for our journey; courage to stand by our convictions; confidence in ourselves; and trust in our Heavenly Father and Savior, Jesus Christ. He fills us with light, truth, and power. He warms our smile, lightens our step, helps us choose correctly, offers protection, and enriches every other aspect of our lives. It is not a slight thing that the Holy Ghost reveals to us personal messages from a loving Heavenly Father. As we let His light in, the Holy Ghost's message can replace any part of us that doubts. I testify that when He whispers of our worth, we should believe Him!

Chapter Eleven
Enough Is Enough

If you want to feel better about yourself, try being grateful for what you have.[56]
—Mindy Raye Friedman

PLEASE PARDON ME FOR STATING the obvious, but life isn't fair. You've no doubt heard that statement before and discovered it for yourself. Even though we know that rationally, we may be frustrated at times by what we perceive as inequities in our lives. The bold new world of Internet connections and instant gratification can fuel the dissatisfaction. A lot of postings on various social media outlets make it seem like so many lives are filled entirely of fantastic vacations, amazing adventures, and lots and lots of wonderful. We should keep in mind that, like a highlight reel, most posts are about the best days. The reality in a complicated world is that everyone experiences opposition and disappointment, whether we hear about it or not.

Negative feelings about ourselves and discontentment with our lives can also arise from seeing what others have and wishing we had more. There are certainly inequities as we look out at the world and others around us, but the quest of our lives is not an accumulation of money, titles, or things. What any of us have that seems more or less than what others have certainly doesn't mean we are more or less loved than someone else. Even as our situations differ, our Heavenly Father loves us equally and blesses us all. The key lies in something Alma expressed long ago: "For I ought to be content with the things which the Lord hath allotted unto me" (Alma 29:3).

When we're tempted to be dissatisfied with what we have or preoccupied with what we don't and it's affecting how we feel about ourselves, God has an answer for us. He expects us to be grateful. He asks us to confess His hand in all things (see D&C 59:21). He must know gratitude improves our outlook, lightens our burdens, and causes us to look beyond ourselves to the positive impact we can make in this world, even if it's just in our corner of it. Gratitude helps us regularly reflect on the good rather than dwelling on perceived deficiencies.

After reading to this point, you may have already realized that I'm not as grateful as I could or should be. Developing more gratitude is something I work at every single day, and I still make so many mistakes. But even as I struggle, I know that when I'm grateful, I feel better about the world, my life, and everyone around me, including myself. I also know gratitude makes it easier for me to more fully recognize my numerous blessings.

Allow me to share an experience from my teen years in which my ingratitude was clearly on display. It is forever etched in my memory. One year for Christmas, I asked for a special gift fairly late in the season. I was in junior high school and had developed an interest in acting that sparked an enthusiasm for all things theatrical. I desperately wanted a director's chair for my room as an expression of that interest. Honestly, I didn't see any reason I wouldn't receive it. Though my parents were not wealthy, they *always* went without for us. I may not have had everything I wanted, but I had everything I needed and much of what I wanted as well.

It was long before the invention of the Internet, or even home computers for that matter, so I was left to thumb through the pages of the old-fashioned JCPenney holiday catalog. Much to my delight, I found the chair of my dreams pictured on one of the pages along with a price that seemed reasonable to my adolescent sensibilities. I don't know that I even considered how many days it was before Christmas or how my mom might have had to scramble to get it in time along with everything else she was doing. Two things I knew strengthened my resolve to acquire it, even if it was an unreasonable request. One: I wanted it. Two: she ordered from the catalog all the time. I showed her the picture and officially added the chair to my list.

On Christmas morning, as was our usual tradition, my siblings and I filed into our front room to see a few unwrapped gifts Santa had set out for us along with our overloaded stockings. Eventually we got to the wrapped presents under the tree. As I glanced around when we first entered the room, I wondered where my handsome yellow chair was hiding. Since it was fairly large, I expected it to be set out assembled with the other presents Santa had left for us. I also figured it wouldn't fit very well under the tree. Still, in the season of hope, I held out some hope that my parents had tucked it away for a special surprise. It wasn't until every present was unwrapped and remnants of paper and curling ribbon were strewn about the room that I realized I wasn't getting that chair. Even though I had received more than enough, I was disappointed. I blurted out without really thinking, "So, where's my director's chair?" I regretted the words the minute they popped out of my mouth, but I couldn't take them back no matter how much I wanted to. I don't remember anything I got that year, and I don't recall much of what happened after that. I still blush with embarrassment when I think about it now. I don't think my dad or mom ever said a word. They didn't have to. I've never forgotten how I felt at what must have seemed to my hardworking parents like such an ungrateful response.

Loving parent that He is, our Heavenly Father has given us so many gifts—blessings that come in all types and sizes. It would be unwise to find ourselves, as I did, thinking we don't have enough or wondering where the rest is. Unfortunately, selfishness and ingratitude are common in a world of instant gratification and entitlement. With the endless possibilities available to us, often right at our fingertips, is enough ever enough?

The type of gratitude that comes from recognizing we have enough is captured in something the Apostle Paul wrote to the Philippians. His message is even more remarkable when we recognize he was in prison at the time he composed it. He wrote, "I have learned, in whatsoever state I am, therewith to be content" (Phil. 4:11). There's that word again. *Content.* The scriptural giants Paul and Alma both shared similar messages because they hold the key to living with gratitude. Contentment is the state of being grateful—the essence of gratitude that springs from recognizing our blessings, whatever our circumstances. It's being happy, satisfied, fulfilled. It's perhaps a step beyond gratitude that takes us to acceptance. Almost like a destination, it's where we live.

One of my children taught me a valuable lesson about living with gratitude when I was having a bad day. Nothing had gone terribly wrong. It was just one of those aggravating, too-much-to-do-and-nothing-is-going-right kind of days we all have now and then. My oldest son, Mason, came home from school and sensed my bad mood immediately. He bravely mustered the courage to ask me if I was okay. I mumbled something that sounded almost like a yes. I think at that point he decided it was best to keep his distance, and that was probably the right move. When ten-year-old Tanner came home from school a while later, he picked up on the atmosphere immediately as well. (It *was* hard to miss.) He asked if I was all right, and I grumbled something back about having a bad day.

"I'm sorry," he said, his deep brown eyes showing how much he meant it. He didn't say anything else, but I could tell he was thinking. He put his coat and backpack away (well, maybe not away, but in the general direction of where they belonged) and got a snack out of the pantry. As he came back to the kitchen, he asked softly, "Mom, what was the best part of your day?"

Tanner wasn't being impertinent. He wasn't trying to teach his much older mother (who should have known better) a lesson. It was a thoughtful, humble, sincere invitation. The minute I heard the question, my cold-as-ice attitude instantly melted away. Nothing about the day had changed, but my mindset did. My son, who is wise beyond his years, had gently encouraged me to forget about the minor things that were troubling me and focus on something better. I answered immediately that his sweet smile was the best part of my day. Mason groaned and rolled his eyes in feigned disgust, but my spirit soared as we laughed together and shared an unforgettable experience. Now every time I'm throwing a tantrum, I try to recall that honest question and gentle suggestion that perhaps life is not quite as bad as I'm making it out to be and that I certainly have more to be grateful for than I'm currently recognizing.

Unfortunately, our hardest days leave us a lot more to deal with than an overbooked schedule or a small stream of unpleasant events. And those types of days don't always miraculously turn around the way mine did that day. Often, they are difficult through and through; no knight in shining armor, no hint of a silver lining. There is no question about it that before we get through this life, we will each have real trials and sometimes even tragedy to face. How do we get through those days? It's something I struggle to put into practice on a regular basis, but one of those transforming principles is gratitude.

I'm often humbled by others who carry unimaginable loads and still manage to be grateful. Most of us know people who are naturally appreciative of everything, even their trials, and they aren't afraid to say it. For me, that would be Michelle. She was a friend and sister in my ward who mastered the art of gratitude and was an incredible example of everything the word represents.

Several years ago, Michelle was diagnosed with breast cancer, which she battled for a very long time. Early in her treatment, I saw her in the grocery store just before the busy holiday season. Though she looked weary and not well, she still had that usual radiant smile on her face. I asked her how she was feeling, and I really wanted to know. We talked a bit about her surgery and subsequent treatment. We didn't visit very long before she mentioned how lucky she was that chemotherapy fell opposite the weeks of Thanksgiving and Christmas. Her non-chemo weeks meant she would feel better to celebrate the holidays with those she loved most. It showed in her eyes and in the way she spoke that she was sincerely grateful for what she often referred to as God's many tender mercies to her. I was speechless and a little ashamed of myself that I often complained about much easier circumstances. Humbled, I was unable to muster much of a reply. As I fought back tears of sympathy for her and regret for my ingratitude, I went on my way to gather my composure. It was a moment I will never forget. In the midst of grueling cancer treatments, Michelle had found a sliver of a silver lining. I learned from her that I can find one in my circumstances too, even if it really takes an effort.

Michelle offered some clues to her approach in facing any type of adversity when she spoke at church one Sunday during her cancer treatments. She defined gratitude as a "magical, miraculous power."[57] She identified levels of gratitude that she had implemented herself. She gently encouraged each of us to try them as well. She outlined four self-explanatory steps. One: recognize blessings. Two: express gratitude. Three: give service. Four: feel grateful during difficulties. Michelle was an excellent teacher by word and deed. She was magnificent at every single one of her steps, which is why she was such an effective teacher. They were the very reason she was able to endure her battle and inspire those around her at the same time.

After a valiant fight and numerous rounds of chemotherapy, Michelle lost her life to cancer. Though she is no longer here with us, the lessons she taught live on in the hearts of those who knew her and were touched on a regular basis by the way she lived. She carried with her a noticeable serenity in difficulty, a positivity and graciousness in her suffering. More than anyone else, I know she lived in thankfulness and contentment, whatever her circumstance, and she expressed it without reservation. She was the personification of what President Uchtdorf taught in his masterful address about gratitude. He said:

> This type of gratitude transcends whatever is happening around us. It surpasses disappointment, discouragement, and despair. It blooms just as beautifully in the icy landscape of winter as it does in the pleasant warmth of summer.
>
> When we are grateful to God *in* our circumstances, we can experience gentle peace in the midst of tribulation. In grief, we can still lift up our hearts in praise. In pain, we can glory in Christ's Atonement. In the cold of bitter sorrow, we can experience the closeness and warmth of heaven's embrace.[58]

Certainly, the highest level of gratitude is thankfulness in the midst of trials, just as Michelle taught. It's easy to lose focus during the times of special concern in our lives because the weight of our burden is heavy and it might

57 Personal notes in possession of the author.
58 Dieter F. Uchtdorf, "Grateful in Any Circumstance," *Ensign*, May 2014, 75.

not seem like there's much to be grateful for. Gratitude at this lofty elevation is not being grateful for things, but it is having an attitude that permeates all that we are because of the overarching belief that everything good in our lives comes from God and that all will eventually be made right because of our Savior, Jesus Christ.

To be clear, being grateful doesn't mean we have to sweep our problems under the rug or operate under the illusion that everything is ideal in order to recognize the blessings in our lives. Sister Lisa Ray Turner said it perfectly. Her thoughts shed a realistic light on what gratitude does for us in times of trouble. "Even when mastered, gratitude does not solve all our problems. It's not a phony Pollyanna attitude of ignoring the blemishes and pain of life, nor is it a selfish, self-aggrandizing attitude. It does not erase grief and hardship, but can make those times easier to bear. It can nourish us spiritually and smooth the jagged edges of our crowded lives."[59]

I believe the type of gratitude my friend Michelle possessed was a gift, a part of who she was from the beginning. That's not to say it was always easy for her because it was more a part of her nature. She suffered tremendously, and I'm certain there were times she didn't feel like being grateful. However, she always chose gratitude in those crucial moments. One day I hope to be just like her. Right now, while I'm pretty good at being grateful when things are going my way, I struggle to find the good in difficult situations. What's the answer for those of us who aren't naturally inclined toward gratitude or seeing the bright side of our trials? It's about developing a grateful heart. We can choose gratitude until we feel gratitude.

A simple way to begin is by identifying the best part of the day, just like my son suggested. Some people do that at mealtime, before family prayer, or in a personal journal. The method is not important, but the end result is. There is no quicker path to gratitude than to recognize and give thanks, rather than focusing on what we don't have or what we want. It isn't automatic, but practice leads to habit, and it eventually gets easier to choose and express gratitude because of the change that has happened in our hearts.

My oldest son, Mason, shared something he learned on his mission from a good sister in one of his areas. We learn in the scriptures that we must endure to the end, and we hear it often in lessons and sermons. It sounds pretty taxing when it's worded that way, and honestly, it can be at times. This inspiring sister had turned that thought around. She said that rather than enduring to the end, she preferred to enjoy to the end! I suspect a grateful heart allowed her to do that.

---

59 Lisa Ray Turner, "The Song of Gratitude," *Ensign*, Jul. 1992, 51.

Another important element of having a grateful heart is offering thanks for the countless blessings in our lives that come to us from God in breathtaking abundance. It's a basic lesson we all learned in childhood and that darling three-year-old Olivia had mastered. Sweet Olivia is the daughter of a friend at work. When she occasionally accompanied her mom to the office and I complimented her pretty blonde hair or her cute shoes, she almost always said "thank you." If she didn't, her mother gently reminded her by asking, "What do you say?" She was taught well that a sincere thank-you indicates we don't take the gift or the giver for granted. Those two words go a long way. They gladden our hearts, and they gladden the giver as well.

Ours is the incredible opportunity to speak to our Heavenly Father through prayer whenever we need to, wherever we are. One essential component of prayer is the offering of appreciation for all He has done for us—saying "thank you," if you will. Those heartfelt expressions come at the beginning of our prayers before we approach Him with our needs.

Mason shared something else with me about gratitude that involved a memorable experience he had during a high school seminary class. One day, his seminary teacher asked him to offer a prayer of appreciation only. On occasion, I have also offered similar prayers that consisted only of the expression of gratitude, but I'm not sure I've encouraged my children to do so. When I do pray that way, I find I'm so used to asking for blessings that it takes an effort not to couple my thanks with an associated request for help. That prayer made an impression on Mason, and he was appreciative of the new perspective. He mentioned that it was different from the prayers he usually said, but it wasn't hard for him. His conclusion makes complete sense since we are so richly blessed that we could easily fill every prayer with thanks alone.

A grateful heart helps us recognize the good and frees us to look for God's many gifts to us. They are everywhere. There are little miracles and tender mercies all around us. A grateful heart allows us to count our blessings—not to keep track or compare but to see and appreciate how often Heavenly Father blesses us because He loves us. It also allows us to more graciously navigate trials and setbacks because we are able to see beyond our circumstances and feel the overriding love and care of our Heavenly Father even when we have heavy burdens to carry.

A grateful heart can't help but cheer and lift us. A grateful heart reflects in our eyes and draws others in. A grateful heart makes us more aware of the needs of others and how we can help. A grateful heart shows in our attitude and positively affects how we see the world, how we view others, and how we feel about ourselves.

It's easy to be self-absorbed in our society today, but we live in a big world, and there are many who suffer, often beyond our comprehension. On the days I struggle the most to carry my individual portion of hardship, if I take off the blinders and open my eyes to see things as they really are (see Jacob 4:13), I will inevitably notice or hear about someone else who has it far worse. As a result, I am always sufficiently humbled as I realize my place in the long line of suffering.

As we open our eyes and hearts, there is evidence of God's love all around us. He is in the rivers and raindrops, the tall trees and vibrant fall leaves, the majestic mountains and rolling green hills. We can see Him in a crystal-blue sky and the powder pink of a glorious sunset. He is in the cry of an infant and the laughter of children, the exuberance of youth and the wisdom of old age. He is in the small mercies and miracles in our lives. What does He ask in return for the blessings He bestows? The answer is simple. He expects us to "live in thanksgiving daily" (Alma 34:38).

One of the biggest lessons of life is to acknowledge that through good times and bad, in feast or famine, triumph or trials, there is always room to be grateful. I suspect that just like everything else God asks of us, the gratitude we express is far more for our benefit and our own growth than it is for His. It's not hard to understand why He wants us to be grateful. When you think about it, what's better for us and our self-esteem? Grumping around complaining about what is lacking in our lives, or being grateful and content with all of God's goodness to us?

Chapter Twelve
Get in, Hold on, Have Fun

We can lift ourselves and others as well when we refuse to remain in the realm of negative thought.[60] —Thomas S. Monson

LIKE SUGAR AND SPICE, MILK and cookies, chocolate and more chocolate, gratitude goes hand in hand with a good attitude. They even rhyme. Though seeing things in a positive light doesn't magically solve all our problems, it can work some magic in our lives.

In addressing a positive outlook, I would never want to add burdens or guilt to anyone who suffers from clinical depression. Certainly, that is not something one can wish away or conquer with a positive attitude alone. The kind of remedy I'm referring to has more to do with the periodic discouragement we all feel from time to time. In these types of situations, a positive outlook means a glass half empty is suddenly half full, lemons turn to lemonade, a bad situation is better, and challenges become opportunities for growth. My youngest son, Tanner, reminded me of that one Monday morning. (Yes, the same little guy who invited me to try gratitude for a change. I told you he was wise beyond his years.)

I arose early to get a good start on the day. The morning was humming along, but Mondays, generally speaking, were not my favorite day of the week, because it meant I was back to work. I appreciate my job, but there is always much to do at home that I haven't crammed into the weekend, and the previous weekend was no different. Contemplating leaving all of it behind and going to the office (or probably, more likely, knowing it would still be there when I got home) was the reason for the hesitation that morning.

When it was time to get the show on the road, I came downstairs for family prayer and was greeted cheerfully by my son, who was ready for me to take him to school. In return, I mustered a half-smile and said with a sigh, "Another day."

60 Thomas S. Monson, "The Divine Gift of Gratitude," *Ensign*, Nov. 2010, 88.

He grinned and replied, "Well, that doesn't sound very optimistic. I like to think of it as another opportunity."

Of course he did! In one simple sentence, Tanner reminded me again that the difference between his outlook and mine wasn't a change in the situation. Rather, it was a minor shift, a tiny adjustment in a viewpoint that involved a more positive way of looking at my world. With very little effort, he had outlined a way for me to turn the day into an opportunity simply by the way I saw it.

Tanner's outlook brings to mind a catchy little promotion on BYUtv that invites viewers to "see the good in the world." Perhaps the slogan refers first to the programming we will find on the channel, but it also seems to invite us to actively look for the positive in a world often filled with negativity and cynicism. The more we practice finding the good in situations and in others, the easier it is to not only see the good but to be part of the good. It's not magical thinking. It's not about ignoring concerns and responsibilities or glossing over what is difficult. Similar to developing "an attitude of gratitude,"[61] it is finding the good in all types of situations. In reality, if we're waiting to have a positive attitude or to feel good about ourselves until everything works out, we might be waiting for a long time.

Good thoughts and a positive outlook can filter into every aspect of our lives. A renowned children's author once wrote, "A person who has good thoughts cannot ever be ugly. You can have a wonky nose and a crooked mouth and a double chin and stick-out teeth, but if you have good thoughts they will shine out of your face like sunbeams and you will always look lovely."[62]

A positive thought can easily turn into a positive expression that changes our outlook completely.

If you were around in the seventies like I was, you may remember they were full of sunny yellow smiley faces and the comment heard at the conclusion of almost every interaction, "Have a nice day." The phrase and face were plastered on T-shirts, notebooks, posters, and greeting cards. (It was the original emoticon.) Somewhere along the way, people must have started getting annoyed by all those pleasant yellow faces and well wishes, because we don't see or hear them as often as we used to. But a smile and a sunny disposition never grow old or go out of style. Of course, it isn't just a smile that constitutes a positive attitude, but it's a very good place to start.

We spend a lot of money on makeup, moisturizers, wrinkle creams, and other things that make us look and feel better. At no cost to us, a smile becomes a manifestation of positive thinking that increases our self-esteem as it plays a

61 Thomas S. Monson, "An Attitude of Gratitude," *Ensign*, Feb. 2000.
62 Roald Dahl, *The Twits* (New York: Alfred A. Knopf, 2002), 9.

role in how we feel about ourselves and our situation. The power of a smile is well-documented. When we give a smile away, we hope to positively affect the recipient, but we should never underestimate the return on our investment.

A complete stranger reminded me of the value of a smile one day when I was driving to work. I was in my car waiting for a space in the flow of traffic in order to make the left-hand turn. She was driving the car coming from the opposite direction. As she passed by, she made eye contact with me and sent a friendly smile my way. I had no idea who she was. I was touched enough by her actions that I found myself wiping away a tear. It was a welcome gift, and I was warmed by it. This simple gesture took no extra time on her part, but I'm convinced she had learned that improving someone else's outlook with this small kindness had a similar effect on her. Most of us have probably been touched in one way or another by the power for good in giving or receiving a smile. Indeed, there is value in a positive attitude that shines from the inside out.

Young and old alike can learn a lesson from the ever-optimistic Snow White, who apparently never had a grumpy moment in her life. After she escaped the Huntsman, who was sent to take her life, she took care of seven little men who made messes and never helped her with her chores. She cooked and cleaned while she tried to evade the evil Queen. With all that unpleasantness in her life, the princess (at least in the Disney version) faced the day with a smile *and* a song. What a multitasker! Even more than that, her attitude was contagious. The birds and other woodland creatures joined in the singing and cleaning with her.

If that's just too much enthusiasm to muster, we can consider instead the advice from President Gordon B. Hinckley. He said, "Go forward in life with a twinkle in your eye and a smile on your face, but with great and strong purpose in your heart."[63] He knew of what he spoke and was an example in word and deed. President Hinckley was always a glass-half-full kind of man, and his enthusiasm was infectious. He continually expressed his faith that things would work out. He persuaded us to keep doing our best. He encouraged us to love life and to look for opportunities. He asked us to "stop seeking out the storms and enjoy more fully the sunlight."[64]

In the famous Broadway musical *Annie*, the main character sings about a smile being the perfect complement to any wardrobe. The indomitable little orphan also reminds us that no matter how dark the day before, the sun will

---

63 Gordon B. Hinckley, "How Can I Become the Woman of Whom I Dream?" *Ensign*, May 2001, 95.

64 Gordon B. Hinckley, "Let Not Your Heart Be Troubled" (Brigham Young University devotional, Oct. 29, 1974); speeches.byu.edu.

come up the next. Trite? Perhaps. True? Absolutely. We sing about it too. In Primary, we raise our voices joyfully about smiles that are like sunshine in the simple little tune with a big message.

> A smile is like the sunshine;
> It brightens up the day.
> It gives the eye a twinkle
> And chases frowns away.[65]

We join in the chorus of our congregations about scattering sunshine[66] and having sunshine in our souls.[67] We read about it and we sing about it, so maybe there is something to be said for letting the sun shine in our lives and sharing that light with others.

The positive approach to life takes mental discipline and flexibility. It doesn't always happen automatically. Just like anything else we master, the more we practice, the more proficient we become. It seems like working hard at being happy is counterintuitive, but happiness does require an effort sometimes, especially when we're not naturally inclined to look for it. Just like gratitude, a good attitude is not always brought about by happenstance; it's a decision, a frame of mind. Though we can't always control what happens to us or around us, we can control our reaction to it. If we think about the people we admire most, they are usually those who maintain a hopeful optimism even amidst hardships.

Our stake had an opportunity a while back to participate in a special conference during which we were privileged to hear from Elder Richard G. Scott. As part of his address, he encouraged us to find something to smile about and offered this advice: "If you want to wake up in the morning guaranteed to have a smile on your face, go to bed with a coat hanger in your mouth."[68] That brought a collective chuckle from the audience, but optimism does allow us to put on a pleasant face in all sorts of situations.

Elder Scott didn't just tell us to be happy. He challenged us to establish a pattern in our lives that promotes happiness. In essence, he encouraged us to make our choices consistent with our beliefs. He didn't promise that life would be perfect if we do or that our days would only be filled with happy

---

65 "A Smile Is like the Sunshine," *Children's Songbook*, 267.

66 See "Scatter Sunshine," *Hymns*, no. 230.

67 See "There Is Sunshine in My Soul Today," *Hymns*, no. 227.

68 Also quoted in Richard G. Scott, "To Live Well," BYU commencement speech, Apr. 21, 2011, speeches.byu.edu/talks/richard-g-scott_to-live-well/.

things and pleasant experiences. In summary, his message was that living what we believe is deeply satisfying and fosters an inner joy and lasting peace that can't be acquired any other way.

The people of Nephi had the right idea, at least for a time. At one point in the Book of Mormon, we read as Nephi laments the treatment he's received at the hands of his older brothers, who despise the idea of following God *and* their younger brother. We've heard them grumble through the entire first book of Nephi. In 2 Nephi, their hatred and murmuring eventually reach epic levels. When Nephi fears for his life, God warns him to flee. He obeys, as Nephi is prone to do, and takes with him anyone else who is willing to follow.

Was everything hunky-dory and flowing with milk and honey for Nephi and the faithful -ites who went with him to that new place? I think not. The scriptures tell us they pitched their tents in the wilderness. God did not lead them to a quaint bed and breakfast with comfy mattresses and crisp, hospital-cornered sheets. (From personal experience, nothing would make me feel less positive about my circumstances than living in a tent in the wilderness.) Their troubles with the Lamanites didn't end with the move either. Even with distance between them, there was always one conflict or another. Nephi describes the necessity of making swords after the pattern of Laban's, evidence they needed weapons for protection from their enemies. Yet Nephi said in that familiar scripture, even as his people were making preparations for war, they "lived after the manner of happiness" (2 Ne. 5:27). He also gives us a clue to their happy state. His people were industrious. They worked and built buildings. They raised flocks and herds and planted seeds. They constructed a temple and worshipped in it. And most of all, they kept the judgements, the statutes, and commandments of God in all things (see 2 Ne. 5:10–11).

The key to their happiness and optimistic outlook, like Elder Scott taught, was directly tied to righteous living even as the threat from the enemy was ever-present. Just as it did for the Nephites, our personal righteousness goes a long way in contributing to our own happiness and optimism. Following God's laws gives us the highest potential for success and safety in this life and creates a harmony within us as we live what we believe. Firmly held beliefs lead to increased confidence, greater purpose in daily living, and deeper meaning in our lives.

What are the answers to the consistent spirituality that brightens our outlook and provides the purpose and commitment to keep us going through all sorts of life's experiences? There is nothing new or earth-shattering here. We've touched on them in previous chapters. They are what we often refer to as the "Sunday School answers," like praying, studying scripture, attending the temple, paying tithes, serving, worshiping on the Sabbath, keeping the commandments, and holding family home evening. We learn about these basic gospel principles all the time for a reason. They are the building blocks of a spiritual life. When we are living in harmony and feeling the Spirit in our lives, we are better able to feel positive about ourselves, our future, and our mission, even when the ups and downs leave us feeling like we have little control over our circumstances and are simply along for the ride.

We live within a few minutes of the largest amusement park in Utah. When our children were younger, they felt slighted if they spent their summer vacation without a visit there. So, during the waning weeks of August, we would usually venture to that local park so they had something to report on those *What I Did This Summer* papers the first days back at school.

I didn't enjoy those trips to the amusement park very much, because I am a big chicken and have been since I was young. I am the ride-my-bike-down-the-hill-with-the-brakes-on type of girl. I much prefer a nice safe museum or tame tourist attraction that doesn't involve being shot into the air like a rocket or dropped at the speed of sound. And I'm only a little ashamed to admit I'm partial to the merry-go-round, with its smooth and steady flow and comforting musical accompaniment. (Honestly, that's the way I like my life too!) For that reason alone, I am no fun at an amusement park, and my children know it. When they were young, it was my job to take the little ones with me to the kiddie rides while the older ones went with their thrill-seeking dad. At one point, even my youngest ceased to humor me, stretching as tall as he could to reach the height requirement for the biggest and scariest rides. Eventually, I was left alone to endure the annual trip with my family of daredevils as they looked for the heart-in-the-throat surprises included with the price of a ticket. It was great fun for them, and that part I enjoyed, but I couldn't even watch them and not worry, especially as they waved to me and wiggled back and forth on the mile-high Ferris wheel.

You'll be happy to know that all was not lost on those annual trips. As an onlooker, I noticed something while I watched and waited. Whether it was in the children's section or on the wildest ride in the park, the operator offered a well-rehearsed line that he or she must have said thousands of times in a season (which applies to my husband's driving as well). In essence, "Get in, hold on, and have fun."

Life, with its twists and turns, is reminiscent of those amusement park rides. Along with exhilarating surprises around unexpected corners, there are also days that have us wondering whether we are coming or going. Sometimes there are uneven spots that jar us or test our stamina or cause us to question who we are. By design, among the amazing days and thrilling opportunities, we are all going to experience opposition, disappointment, and heartache. With its inherent ups and heart-stopping drops, life is more like a roller-coaster than the pleasant, measured bumps of the merry-go-round—the real trick is to hold on and enjoy the ride.

Chapter Thirteen
Longing for Home

*Greater personal spirituality yields greater confidence. . . . Spiritual strength
yields a confidence that cannot be obtained in any other way.*[69]
—Brent L. Top and Bruce A. Chadwick

HAVE YOU EVER BEEN HOMESICK? It seems no matter where we travel or how
long we are away, there is a part of us that longs to be home. Those sentiments
have been echoed through the ages. I remember the days of embroidered
home-sweet-home or home-is-where-the-heart-is samplers hanging on a
kitchen wall. And Dorothy, lost in the Land of Oz, only wants to go home.

I'm not sure I've suffered from the real homesickness I saw a time or two
in my friends at summer camp or school band trips. I understand it, though,
that longing for home. When I was young, my family took a long road trip
almost every summer. We always had the best time! But even though we were
all together, there was something special about pulling back into our driveway.
I can still hear my sweet mom saying at the conclusion of those trips, "Oh, it's
so good to be home."

I remember feeling some pangs of a different type of homesickness at
girls' camp one year. If you've ever been to girls' camp, you know there is
something special that happens there in nature and under the stars that sparks
the embers of faith and testimony. I had one such experience as a stake visitor
in a ward camp testimony meeting many years ago. It was the last night of
camp at the culmination of all those fun and spiritual experiences that had
happened throughout the week. Even though I had only been there a day, I
could hear and feel the spiritual impact of those experiences as I listened to
sweet testimonies. As the meeting drew to a close, and because of the strong

---

69 Brent L. Top and Bruce A. Chadwick, "Helping Children Develop Feelings of Self-
    Worth," *Ensign*, Feb. 2006, 35.

spirit, I sensed a powerful connection to my heavenly home. I was concerned about some personal health problems at the time and had a longing to reach out, to feel the encouragement and comfort of my Eternal Father. In nature and under the stars He created, He was near me and wrapped me in the arms of His unending love and compassion.

Though we are a long way from home, our Heavenly Father didn't send us here to flounder on our own. He knew we would need some assistance to make it safely through our mortal experience. Building on Elder Scott's advice from the previous chapter of establishing a pattern of happiness in our lives, we learn that consistently living spiritual principles enables us to find meaning, direction, and the lasting joy our Heavenly Father wants for all His children. The things that fill our souls and make us complete are accumulated through righteous living one drop at a time. To successfully navigate this life, we need the type of spiritual strength that contributes to an abiding sense of our eternal worth and reminds us of eternal connections.

There are numerous components of spirituality, and we've previously addressed several of them. However, any list would be incomplete without three elements, important on their own, but that, in harmony, create a spiritual wholeness and beauty that shine within us and light our way. They are personal prayer, scripture study, and temple attendance.

I learned something about the impact that practicing one aspect of the gospel has on another from eleven-year-old Spencer when he gave a talk in Primary using a bread-making analogy. His mother taught him to add a little sugar to the yeast. Of course, the yeast will work on its own, but the dough rises higher with the sugar-and-yeast combination than with just yeast alone. Similarly, when we strive to live the principles of the gospel in combination, our own spirituality is enhanced. The regular practice of prayer, scripture study, and temple attendance is beneficial to our growth and to our relationship with our Heavenly Father and Savior, Jesus Christ. Each is a source of peace and happiness on its own. However, when we have a special need, an earnest desire, or an important decision or question, using these three elements in tandem often allows for the guidance and influence we seek in important and powerful ways. An extra emphasis so often facilitates the clarity we seek, particularly as we add to the mix the special ingredient of fasting. The spiritual manifestations we receive as a result lead to a firmer belief, to faith in ourselves and especially in our Savior, Jesus Christ, as well as an increased awareness of the close proximity of our heavenly home.

Prayer was long ago established as our channel of communication with God. He is always there for us when we reach out to Him. I felt the significance of what that constant availability means in a personal way one day when my daughter tried to reach me. First of all, I should disclose that I don't have a cell phone. Really! As you might imagine, there are some benefits of not having a personal cellular device, like being able to finish a transaction without dirty looks from sales clerks and not interrupting during sacrament meeting when we forget to turn it off. Alas, there are some downsides too.

Several years ago, I had the use of a cell phone for a short period of time. Because I was unaccustomed to carrying it around, I didn't usually notice when the silly thing rang. To accommodate the complaints of loved ones who still couldn't get ahold of me, even with a cell phone, I set the ring to a more intrusive Latin beat. That wasn't the answer either. The music coming from my purse often startled me since I didn't always recognize it immediately. Consequently, I still usually didn't get to the phone in time. Among all my cell-phone shortcomings though, the biggest by far is that I am a failure at texting, which is practically a crime in this era of technology.

My ineptitude posed a huge problem the day I got a text from my daughter Chelsey, who was in high school at the time. Out of the blue, my phone buzzed and the message, "R U there?" popped up on the screen. (It was one of the abbreviations in text vernacular I actually understood.) *Yes, I'm here*, I thought. I *was* there at the other end of the phone, and I read her text seconds after she sent it. I knew she was in class and getting caught certainly meant that her teacher would confiscate the phone. Since that was a fate worse than death, I figured it had to be an emergency. What I couldn't figure out was how to respond. After several unsuccessful attempts to send a simple answer back, I enlisted the help of a much younger, more connected coworker. Unfortunately, by that time, Chelsey wasn't waiting for my answer anymore. When she finally reached my landline between classes, she wondered why I hadn't responded to her text. I learned she was sick and needed to be excused from class. I felt terrible that she was miserable for the better part of an hour waiting for my response.

With the world at our fingertips, it's hard to fathom waiting for messages from anyone, let alone via carrier pigeon, Pony Express, or the arrival of the stagecoach like they used to do. One of the best things about our various communication options is that when we reach out to make a connection, others are able to respond, sometimes instantaneously. Long before technology got us to this place of incredible convenience, another type of instant messaging has ever been available to communicate with our Heavenly Father. The direct line to Him is always open. That's not to say that every prayer will be answered immediately or exactly as we prefer, but He is steady and constant and there for us whenever, wherever we need Him.

Through regular prayer, we draw closer to God, enabling us to realize the difference between saying prayers and accessing the power of prayer in our lives. If we're offering prayers on an irregular basis, we may be less comfortable in approaching Him like we might be when greeting an old acquaintance we haven't spoken to in a while. The Bible Dictionary gives us some additional insight, as follows: "As soon as we learn the true relationship in which we stand toward God (namely, God is our Father, and we are His children), then at once prayer becomes natural and instinctive on our part (Matt. 7:7–11). Many of the so-called difficulties about prayer arise from forgetting this relationship."[70]

When we are consistent in our prayers, we increase in confidence to "come boldly unto the throne of grace, that we may obtain mercy, and find grace to help in time of need" (Heb. 4:16). We are also comfortable asking for the help we need and offering gratitude and devotion. We are invited to seek help for our individual concerns through prayer. The answers will come in a personal way, specific to our circumstances, as we diligently seek them.

Even if we've been away, we never need worry that we are strangers to God. As a loving parent, He knows us better than we know ourselves. He wants us to come to Him, to confide in Him. No matter the length of time that passes between our communications, He is still there. If we sense a distance, it is on our part, not His. Prayer is our lifeline to our Heavenly Father and is a key to our sense of worth and spiritual preparation.

Added to prayer, scripture study becomes another powerful element to maintaining a steady sense of self and strengthening our spiritual reserves. Rosalie shared some touching thoughts about the impact of the scriptures in her life during a testimony meeting in our ward. As a ninth-grader, she had just started seminary. After the first day of class, she realized she would need a different set of scriptures than the ones she used for study at home. When she asked if there were some others she could use, her mom handed her a well-worn set of family scriptures. Rosalie reported that she was disappointed when she first saw them because they weren't in very good shape. She even thought to herself, *Oh great. Beat-up scriptures!*[71] Because of the condition they were in, she wasn't very enthusiastic about using them for seminary. Despite her apprehension, she took them, and through the year, she came to realize just how special they are. She said she loves to see the passages other family members have highlighted. And she hopes one day her scriptures will be as used and marked as those family scriptures. Rosalie discovered that the scriptures don't wear out or become less valuable because the cover is scuffed or the pages are ragged or torn. The more

70   Bible Dictionary, "Prayer."
71   Personal notes in possession of the author.

we wear out the pages by studying them, marking our favorite passages, writing in the margins, and referring to them over and over again, the more valuable they become.

Though we may not always think of scripture study as an essential part of our pursuit to a steady self-esteem, it can certainly contribute as we look for messages of worth and internalize what we read. Sister Ardeth Kapp, former General President of the Young Women, often refers to the scriptures in a personal way. She said, "The holy scriptures are like letters from home telling us how we can draw near to our Father in Heaven."[72] Even with all our electronic communication options, there is nothing quite like receiving personal correspondence through the mail, especially amidst all the bills and junk mail. When we think of the holy scriptures the same way we view a letter from a loved one, it's not just about reading the words; it's about joining us in a bigger way to our Heavenly Father and Jesus Christ, who have an active interest in our lives.

How many scriptures address our worth? I don't really know. In a way, I suppose they all do. We don't have to look very far to find references that speak directly of the kind of love that surpasses our understanding. The words of John tell us, "For God so loved the world, that he gave his only begotten Son" (John 3:16). In Romans, we read, "Nor height, nor depth, nor any other creature, shall be able to separate us from the love of God, which is in Christ Jesus our Lord" (Rom. 8:39). And Nephi testifies, "My God hath been my support; he hath led me through mine afflictions in the wilderness; and he hath preserved me upon the waters of the great deep. He hath filled me with his love" (2 Ne. 4:20–21). Those are just a few examples. We can find numerous additional personal messages in the scriptures, as well as the specific direction we need in order to live in such a way to continually feel God's love and an assurance of our value to Him.

Regular temple attendance rounds out the trio. There is no better place to feel the love of God and to be reminded of all He has in store for us than in the temple. Being in or near the temple is the closest thing to heaven on this earth. It is a holy place—a haven—that affirms our worth and ties us to our Heavenly Father and all those we love who have gone on before us. It clears away the fog and confusion by reminding us of our eternal nature.

I was in a bit of a fog myself as I made my way to the beautiful Bountiful Utah Temple one weekday morning before I reported to work. I looked forward to the sweet solace I knew I would find there that morning, and it was especially needed. Ironically, a typical January inversion had rolled out its vast

---

72   Ardeth G. Kapp, "The Holy Scriptures: Letters from Home," *Ensign*, Nov. 1985, 95.

winter blanket across the Wasatch Front. Though fog isn't unusual in northern Utah, this time it had stayed too long. As I left early for the temple, the sun struggled to slip through the layers of gray. Because of my gloomy mood, I was silently rooting for its welcome rays to break through. Alas, my cheers were to no avail. By the time I got to the freeway, the dismal mist had completely engulfed the sun again.

The temple is strikingly situated on a hill above Bountiful, Utah. Everything in the valley was covered with fog, but as I took the freeway exit and started my ascent to the temple, I was pleased to see that the haze had dispersed ever so slightly. By the time I reached the temple parking lot, the sun's brightness there had penetrated a brilliant-blue day. It wasn't that the fog had lifted. I could see it still clinging stubbornly to rooftops and roadways below. Fittingly, the temple stood above the fog.

We needed a powerful storm to clear the thick inversion in the valley. That day the temple was the answer to my personal inversion. As I walked through the temple doors, I was greeted by friendly workers. In the chapel, the organ music added to the reverence and quiet reassurance I felt there. The stained-glass windows in the hallway stretched toward heaven vertically, letting the light in and warming my soul. In the session itself, the sweet feelings of peace returned as the fog lifted and my cloudy vision cleared.

Each time we attend the temple, the sacred covenants and ordinances invite us to rise above our earthly experience, helping us see ourselves the way our Father does. What we learn there enables us to look past the finite issues that limit our vision as we catch a glimpse of forever. As the worldly haze disperses, everything about the temple reminds us of our eternal relationship to God and of our great worth.

If you can't currently go to the temple or are working toward that day, keep striving. If you are close enough to a temple to visit, even spending time near the temple is a blessing. We can feel the presence of the Spirit as we seek the temple when we have questions or need direction, even when we don't go inside. The era of temple building has enabled easier access for many who have always dreamed of going. If you don't live near enough to visit often, placing temple pictures in your home is a reminder of the desire to partake of sacred covenants and ordinances there.

Prayer, scripture study, and temple blessings are all gifts from a loving Father and are a powerful influence in our lives as they remind us of our eternal connection to Him. Those connections lead to greater confidence as we increase in faith and obedience. When we love and live what we know, we gain faith in ourselves and confidence in our ability to make important decisions. Living gospel principles and keeping covenants keeps us firmly planted and moving forward on the straight and narrow path, which leads to comfort and sweet assurance in ourselves and in the understanding that our heavenly home isn't very far away.

Chapter Fourteen
The Color of Service

The worth of souls is indeed great in the sight of God. Ours is the precious privilege, armed with this knowledge, to make a difference in the lives of others.[73]
—Thomas S. Monson

IF SERVICE WERE A COLOR, what color would it be? Maybe for you it's a soft green or pastel blue. Perhaps it's a dazzling purple or vibrant orange. For a very long time, service was always yellow to me because of the bright, sunny way serving makes me feel. Many years ago, a significant experience at Christmastime meant from that time on, service would forever be red.

My husband had been out of work for a while, and due to the financial setbacks, we weren't making ends meet. Christmas was fast approaching, and I was afraid it was going to skip us that year. It's not that we really needed anything. We already had so much. But I didn't want the holiday to pass my children by completely, and I secretly hoped there was some way to pull off a little bit of magic for them. The generosity and love of family members and anonymous friends in our neighborhood and ward meant I didn't wait or wonder very long. Because of them, we had a modest Christmas that year, and it was one of our most memorable yet.

The miracle began in early December when we received two generous gifts of money, one from some dear family members and the other delivered to us by our good bishop. He told us the undisclosed giver had stipulated we use it however we choose. Among other kindnesses, an anonymous friend left a package of new stockings for my boys, along with a box and card addressed to me. The sweet note offered words of encouragement about our situation. With tears streaming down my face, I opened the package and discovered a beautiful red wool jacket that was just my size.

---

73 Thomas S. Monson, "To Learn, to Do, to Be," *Ensign*, Nov. 2008, 61.

Anyone who has endured difficulty in this life (and that would be all of us) understands it's not only the physical toll that hardship takes. We are often spiritually and emotionally impacted as well. Due to the circumstances, I wasn't in a great place in any of those areas. That red jacket quickly became a symbol of service and Christlike love because of all the good people around me who lifted my spirits and helped me keep going, even if I didn't always know who they were.

Prior to that December, red had never been my go-to color. However, I wore the jacket that year and at Christmastime ever since with a grateful heart. Though many years have passed since then, every time I see the red jacket in my closet or wear it now, I am flooded with memories of the generosity and sweet acts of service that came to us in a remarkable way and really saved our family that Christmas. The kind acts of many have proved to me through the years that, "God does notice us, and he watches over us. But it is usually through another person that he meets our needs."[74]

The ironic thing about service is that in the giving of ourselves, we are not lessened or depleted in any way. It's not that we won't be tired or maybe even exhausted after we serve, but in a very real way, we are also lifted, filled, and renewed. In addition, serving helps us feel better about ourselves and our circumstances. President Spencer W. Kimball said, "The more we serve our fellowmen in appropriate ways, the more substance there is to our souls. We become more significant individuals as we serve others. We become more substantive as we serve others—indeed, it is easier to 'find' ourselves because there is so much more of us to find!"[75]

Why does service have that effect on us? Perhaps it's partly because the Savior has told us that serving our fellow men is a partnership with Him. We are carrying out His work, and in so doing we are serving Him and trying to do what He would do if He were here. It is also often a relief to think less about our own concerns and focus our attention on someone else. When we serve, we generally have the opportunity to notice what others are going through. In comparison, we often feel like our own burdens aren't quite as heavy, or at the very least, we recognize through similar shared experiences that we are not in this alone. As we serve, our burdens are lifted in a miraculous way.

Many times, when we are called on to help, we may be in more difficult circumstances ourselves. Elder Neal A. Maxwell shared this thought: "So often our sisters comfort others when their own needs are greater than those being comforted. That quality is like the generosity of Jesus on the cross. Empathy

---

74 Spencer W. Kimball, "Small Acts of Service," *Ensign*, Dec. 1974, 2.
75 *Teachings of Presidents of the Church: Spencer W. Kimball* (2006), 85–86.

during agony is a portion of divinity!"[76] The Savior set the example for us, and He knows more about agony than anyone who ever lived. Even a portion—a tiny sliver—of that divinity is something to earnestly seek and will be a blessing in our own lives and in the lives of others.

If we are His followers, we will strive to serve our fellow men. Just like everything else He asks of us, the personal blessings we receive far outweigh anything we give away. When we are tired, when we are discouraged, when we are lacking confidence or feeling bad about ourselves, one of the best remedies is right at our fingertips. We don't have to look very far to find someone in need.

Sister Chieko Okazaki, former second counselor in the general Relief Society presidency, spoke at a women's gathering in my area many years ago. One statement she made impacted me more than any other. In speaking about what we can do to help others, she suggested that service wasn't always about casseroles. That comment puzzled me at first, and I felt a little guilty, though I'm sure it wasn't her intent. As I thought about what she said, I had to acknowledge that my service was almost always about casseroles because most of the time I didn't have a clue what else to do. Her suggestion opened my mind to possibilities and resulted in a greater awareness on my part about all the good that was happening around me. Through the years I've come to understand, mostly through watching others, that sometimes service *is* a casserole and sometimes it's something else.

Years ago, when I was down with a difficult pregnancy, there were many amazing examples of what Sister Okazaki meant. Our family received service then as a casserole or a pizza or a pan of lasagna. And it was so needed. Members of the Relief Society in our ward brought meals to us twice a week until I was well enough to prepare them again myself. I don't know what we would have done without the kind of help that nourished bodies and spirits too. We also received service in many other ways. Jackie stopped by one day and offered an hour to run some long-overdue errands. She bought milk and postage stamps and dropped some payments in the mail. Debbie brought yarn and a pattern for a beautiful blanket that I could crochet and use when we blessed the baby we were waiting for. Tam was tireless in the service she rendered throughout the pregnancy. Along with the many other acts of love and compassion she rendered, she learned some medical procedures just in case my husband wasn't around when I needed help. Lisa and Melinda planted beautiful flowers. Maureen came by to talk. The Primary presidency helped the children tie a quilt for me. The whole group delivered it and sang favorite Primary songs to me that brightened my day and touched my heart. My mom stayed and cared

76 Neal A. Maxwell, "The Women of God," *Ensign*, May 1978, 10.

for me and my family for several months until I was back on my feet. My dad drove her back and forth at the beginning and end of each week. My husband changed IV bags and took care of everything else. The list of all that was done for us is incredible and practically endless. Though we desperately needed the help, all that receiving wasn't easy, partly because it meant a position of vulnerability for me, but especially because I knew that many who came to my rescue had challenges of their own. There were also many others who made my life easier and offered love and support. Each individual act of service carried us during that difficult time.

I've learned from observation that there are willing souls who drop everything when they see or sense a need. They are an inspiration to me. I'm not very spontaneous, so spur-of-the-moment service doesn't often fit into my plans. I've been guilty at least a time or two of not entering the opportunity with as generous a heart as I should, which isn't the right approach since people seldom know beforehand when they might require some help. Those in need aren't able to plan their crises to meet my schedule or to fit into a convenient slot on my calendar, preferably with at least a few days of warning. I'm trying to overcome my inflexibility and do better. While I have a long way to go, I learn every day from examples all around me of better people who are always there to lend a hand at a moment's notice and who seem to inherently know what to do.

One of those people was a sweet sister in my stake. Along with exercise, personal prayer, and scripture study, she always said her best days incorporated service. She wasn't any less busy than I was. She simply made time to add service to each day. Another sister on my visiting teaching route recently told me her husband prayed every morning for an opportunity to serve. If we desire to serve and ask for the opportunity, God will provide the way, even if it is just a simple act.

We shouldn't be afraid to leave the cleaning or other projects behind if we're needed somewhere else. Heaven knows it will all be there when we get home. We can follow our hearts and do our part to lift another's burdens and in so doing, lift a portion of our own burdens as well. Likewise, we shouldn't worry because we feel our contribution is small. What we have to offer might be exactly what someone else needs. We could very well be the answer to a prayer. In addition, we don't need to get caught up in all the details of the perfect service project to render aid.

In the *Do not as I do* category, sometimes I spend so much time trying to figure out the right thing to do that the opportunity for service nearly passes me by. By way of a not-so-admirable example, several years ago a friend of mine was by her young son's side for several days at the hospital following a serious accident he'd had. I wanted to take some homemade cookies and other snacks to the hospital since she and her family were there almost all the time. On the day I decided to deliver the food, I spent so much time looking for just the right basket to put the food in that I nearly didn't make it to the hospital. I knew it was silly, but that didn't stop me. I was frantic by the time I found just the right basket, and I nearly missed visiting hours. Fingers crossed that intent actually counts for something, but please don't make the same mistakes I do. We needn't be concerned about having everything wrapped up and tied with a bow in order to serve. Even when all we can think to do involves a casserole, it's the *service* that counts!

We might equate service with big projects and lots of planning, and sometimes that's the case, but there are also numerous simple acts of service that can be done almost without thinking. The list is long and far-reaching—letting someone ahead of us in a line, waving to a neighbor, reading to a child, sending a thank-you note, forgiving someone, saying something nice about someone else, sending a letter to someone we admire, listening without interrupting, giving up a good parking spot, leaving a treat for the mail carrier, etcetera. In addition, we don't always think of the work we do in our families or our callings as service, but the things we do for them, large or small, certainly qualify.

In the end, each good deed is rewarded, though it doesn't always come back to us immediately, tangibly, or perhaps at all in this life. So often, the reward isn't something the one we serve returns to us. The real and most valuable compensation is in the way we feel and especially in the Christlike attributes we expand each time we serve. Of course, the best motivation for our good works is not the thought of reward but the desire to help, the yearning to be more like our Savior, the love we feel from Him in our lives, and the increase of love we have for others.

Jesus said, "Give and it shall be given unto you; good measure, pressed down, and shaken together, and running over. . . . For with that same measure that ye mete withal it shall be measured to you again" (Luke 6:38). Let's consider that scripture in baking terms, since that's what the words bring to mind. Imagine a recipe calls for a cup of packed brown sugar. First, we fill the measuring cup to the brim. Then we press it firmly into the cup. As we compact the brown sugar, it's a baking truth that there is always room for more. That's how our Heavenly Father blesses us as we serve each other, even to overflowing.

One of the simplest ways we can serve is by being kind. There are those today who would mistake kindness for weakness, but that is simply not the case. Consider that Jesus Christ is omnipotent, yet one of His special attributes is His loving kindness. When I hear the stories of Jesus, I am always touched by the tender account of Mary and Martha at the death of their beloved brother Lazarus. The worried sisters were close friends of the Savior, and believers. They knew of His power and how much He loved Lazarus too, so they sent for Him while Lazarus was still sick. By the time Jesus arrived, their brother had already been dead four days. Mary and Martha were grieving and overcome with sorrow. We understand from leading verses that on His way to a miracle, Jesus already knew and had shared with His Apostles that He would raise Lazarus from the dead as a testament to His healing power. Knowing this, what did Jesus do when He talked with Mary and Martha? He didn't dismiss their concerns or make light of their tears. He wept with them (see John 11:1–35).

The scriptures are replete with examples of kindness Jesus showed in all sorts of situations. He sought the friendless, the outcast, and the downtrodden. He comforted and healed the sick. He fed His followers with the good word of God and also with loaves and fishes when they were hungry, instead of sending them away. His life leaves no doubt that kindness in action is at the very core of service and is at the heart of the gospel of Jesus Christ.

The word *kindness* itself is bright and cheerful, like a breath of fresh air. When we think about synonyms for kindness, we find a sermon in every word: courtesy, compassion, decency, charity, gentleness, graciousness, helpfulness, patience, sweetness, tenderness, generosity, humanity, sympathy, thoughtfulness, tolerance, understanding, unselfishness, consideration, goodness, hospitality, mildness, and mercy.

Showing kindness may be simple, but the result of being kind is far-reaching and full of meaning, encompassing a lot of human behavior and touching hearts. In a perfect world, our kindness would be met with kindness. But even when it isn't, we should still be kind.

With Jesus Christ showing the way, as we reach out to those in need, they can feel His love and the love of our Heavenly Father through us, which feels like a little bit of heaven on this earth. There is nothing better for our sense of worth than that! As we extend our hands and hearts toward others in Christlike service, something wonderful also happens inside. Our own spirits are lightened and healed. We become more refined. We are stronger, happier, more compassionate, more peaceful, more resilient, and more receptive to the whisperings of the Holy Spirit.

Chapter Fifteen
How Does Your Garden Grow?

I am convinced that when we obtain a witness of who we really are and possess healthy feelings of self-worth because of it, our joy in the accomplishments of others is magnified.[77] —Glenn L. Pace

OF ALL THE NURSERY-RHYME CHARACTERS I remember from my childhood, I just might admire Mary the most. Sure, she was contrary, but she also had a green thumb, which I do not. Though I come from a long line of talented gardeners, I am not horticulturally gifted in the least. While gardening comes naturally to so many of my family members, I have to work hard at it, and my plants suffer. Many a plant has met its demise at my hands, and I really admire anyone who can successfully grow silver bells, cockle shells, or anything else.

In addition, Mary also had the right idea in selecting more than one type of flower to plant. The most awe-inspiring gardens are those filled with plants and flowers of variety, that complement each other. During the time I was down with my difficult pregnancy, I learned something valuable about all sorts of growing things.

I'd like to say the bed-rest imposed by my complications was the reason my enormous flower bed was filled only with dirt. It wasn't. I actually had no business having a garden space as big as the one in my front yard. It had never been planted in all the years we had lived in our home, for one reason alone—plants come to my home to die. Luckily for me, two lovely friends took it upon themselves to transform the dirt into a lovely flower garden as a service to me and my family.

Several months into this challenging pregnancy, on one lovely late spring morning, I looked out my front room window at the clear sky and warm sun and longed to be outside. I was also longing for some company when I noticed

77 Glenn L. Pace, "Confidence and Self-Worth," *Ensign*, Jan. 2005, 35.

Lisa and Melinda in my front yard. At first I wasn't sure why they were there. It didn't take long to notice they had several flats of flowers that were certainly not there when they'd come. They worked together preparing the barren ground and slipping the plants into pockets of soil. Unbeknownst to them, I watched them from the window for some time, tears on my face and a heart full of love and gratitude. Their act of love was the service that kept on serving. The flowers they planted brought me great joy that day and every other day until the frost came. Thoughts of these sisters' actions continued to warm my heart during the cold months of winter until the birth of my son. To this day, I think about their service and I'm filled with an overwhelming sense of appreciation.

Lisa and Melinda left little markers beside the flowers they planted so I would know what they were and how to care for them. I saved them for a while, long after the flowers were gone. That day was engraved on my heart, and I didn't want to forget. Sadly, I've since lost track of the plastic tags, and I can't recall now what flowers grew in that beautiful garden they planted for me then. However, I will never forget their generosity and how splendidly everything bloomed together, brightening my days and my yard.

Lisa told me later, almost apologetically, that since it was late in the season she'd had to be creative with her selection due to the limited availability at the greenhouse. Of course, there was no apology necessary, and there was nothing lacking in what she had chosen! Every single flower brought its own beauty in a way that was unexpected and absolutely lovely.

Just like the flowers, the two sweet sisters who planted them were special and unique in their own way, as are all women. God made us in different varieties, each one as beautiful as the next, each adding her own individuality and flair. Being secure in ourselves allows us to recognize our own worth as well as the worth of each of our sisters because we understand that He loves us all. We've talked about heavenly grandstands cheering us on, but we can each be part of some earthly grandstands as well. We can form a chorus of women, cheering for each other, celebrating each another, and learning from, loving, and lifting each other.

One of the best parts of serving in various organizations in the Church is the opportunity to better know those with whom we serve. Due to callings through the years, in addition to the exemplary spirituality they each possess, I learned that Kathy is marvelously creative and has an eye for lovely things. Vicki has a wonderful way with words, and her poetry is out of this world. Jan is talented at decorating and can create something amazing from nothing. Liz has impressive speaking and leadership abilities. Tam is imaginative and can present a Primary sharing time beyond compare and will drop everything to help at a moment's notice. Annette is smart, capable, and organized. Paula is kind and sweet and supportive. Annie is insightful, accepting, and wise, and the list goes on and on. Of course, the amazing and notable qualities in these women aren't limited to what I've listed here. In fact, a lot of their talents and abilities overlap, but each woman is different, and I've learned invaluable lessons from every single one. There are things I've learned from too many women to mention inside and outside of Church service. I'm a better person for knowing them, and I've personally benefited from the qualities and attributes they possess.

Mosiah instructed his people that their hearts should be "knit together in unity and in love" (Mosiah 18:21). He must have known that we are stronger when we stand together than when we stand alone. A long time ago, Sister Lucy Mack Smith told the women of Nauvoo, "We must cherish one another, watch over one another, comfort one another and gain instruction that we may all sit down in heaven together."[78] If that was true of her time, it is doubly true today. There is enough division in the world, enough disparaging, comparing, and contention.

I've watched with great admiration as my oldest daughter, Whitney, cares for her young family. She is a wonderful and patient mother. As her little ones are just learning to talk, she says, "Use your words," to encourage them to tell her what they need rather than pointing or grunting or gesturing. No matter how long we've been using our words to communicate, they not only express what we want or need but they can also have an impact for good or ill on those who hear them.

Perhaps you've noticed in our society today that civility is slipping, and speaking one's mind no matter the cost to another has become a popular trend. Some even tout the idea that it's good for us to *always* say exactly what we think. Others believe it's unhealthy to keep our thoughts and opinions to ourselves. Much of how society communicates today is done through social media and via comments on articles and other sources of information found online. Sometimes the hostility and criticism are too personal and are taken beyond the extreme. In these situations, we almost find it necessary to avert our eyes, much as we would an accident we would rather not see.

My daughter recently told me about something that went on in one of those virtual gathering places. A friend of hers had innocently posted on her own page within a popular networking site some information about

---

78 *Daughters in My Kingdom: The History and Work of Relief Society* (2011), 25.

something that had happened in her life that day. She wasn't complaining, and she wasn't commenting about someone else. She wasn't taking a stand. She hadn't committed a crime. She hadn't asked for opinions. As an adult, she merely mentioned a decision she'd made that was hers alone to make. The result of that innocent post? She was blasted by derogatory comments, opinions, and insults. There were remarks that friends and strangers as well would have never dreamed of saying to her face, or at least I'd like to hope that's the case. It was disheartening, to say the least.

The Internet is a whole new frontier that has made it possible to communicate in ways we never have before. There are nameless, faceless opportunities to insult and put down at every turn. But just because everyone else seems to be doing it doesn't mean we have to get involved. It's like an old analogy that suggests that words are like feathers in the wind. Once they're out, we can never gather them back. Whenever I heard that analogy in Church or my seminary class, I used to picture it like fluffy pillow fights, feathers flying everywhere. With our high-tech society and the rapid pace at which things spread, it's true that words, like feathers, are harder to contain than ever before, but feathers are light and soft. It might be better to picture prickly barbs or metal shards aloft to give a more accurate visual of what harsh words can do. Additionally, what is posted online today can travel around the world and back in no time at all and can impact people negatively or positively in a way that has never before been possible.

As members of Jesus Christ's Church, we simply must hold ourselves to a higher standard. When our leaders ask us to join in the discussion,[79] they expect us to be civil and respectful. If we have a difference of opinion, we should temper our comments and share our views in a way that isn't an attack, if we need to share them at all. We are all here trying to learn and grow. Not everyone is in the same place. It's not our responsibility to point out the weaknesses we perceive in others, to focus on the negative, or to scrutinize personal decisions. We are warned in the scriptures about seeing the mote in another's eye when we have a beam in our own (see Matt. 7:3). We must remember most of all that real people are behind the things we read and hear, even though we can't see them. There may be times it's necessary for us to address concerns and voice an opinion to those who are within our stewardship, but we need a position of love, trust, or respect in the receiver's life to have the standing to comment in a personal way, and even then, it should be carefully done.

Sometimes emotions run high. We all make mistakes and say things we shouldn't—things we later regret. In those situations, we can accept responsibility,

---

79 See M. Russell Ballard, "Sharing the Gospel Using the Internet," *Ensign*, Jul. 2008, 61–63.

humbly apologize, and earnestly seek forgiveness from the one we have injured. As a general rule, our words should lift, build, encourage, inspire, and testify, not demean or tear down. And just because we can sit unseen behind a computer screen and engage in an unbecoming conversation doesn't mean we should. Contrary to the mantra of many, we simply do not need to say everything that is on our minds. When we feel compelled to take a stand or make a comment, we must first consider the effect our words might have on the real person who is left to endure the uninvited barrage.

As a guide for our conversations, online or otherwise, Sister Lyn Austin shared a formula for determining when to say or not say something. She said, "Before saying anything to anyone, ask yourself three things: Is it true? Is it kind? Is it necessary? If it doesn't meet all three requirements, don't say it."[80] Hers is a simple and effective method for determining whether something we say to others or post online is appropriate. We don't have to agree with everything that's out there or share everyone else's opinions, but we certainly don't have to get involved with the public shaming and inappropriate conversation that often goes on in our world today. Sometimes, when someone expresses an opinion that is different than our own, it is still best to remain silent.

My husband's mother often borrowed a line from Walt Disney's version of *Bambi* when something unkind rolled off her children's tongues. In the movie, after the young bunny Thumper says something unkind about Bambi, the baby fawn, his mother reminds him of what he's probably heard dozens of times. "If you can't say somethin' nice, don't say nothin' at all."[81] But my mother-in-law didn't just say it. She practiced it and set the example for her children. In all the years I knew her, I never heard her say a negative word about anyone. With all the openness and vast avenues of communication available to us today, it might seem like an old-fashioned approach. But it is still true that an elevated way of speaking uplifts us and others.

Turning our focus away from less-than-pleasant aspects of social media and other Internet forums, there's so much good that comes from them as well. They are instrumental in the fulfilling of the glorious promise that the gospel will flood the earth. We can be part of a force for good and reach people we never have before. We can share thoughts and experiences that uplift and inspire. We can post encouraging comments and ideas that coincide with our values.

Just as we should often choose to remain silent if we don't have something nice or respectful to say, we should not remain silent when we have the

80 Lyn Austin, "A Hard Look at Myself," *Ensign*, Feb. 1990, 64.
81 *Bambi*, directed by David Hand (Walt Disney, 1947).

opportunity to use words to praise and encourage others. One of my favorite thoughts on the matter comes from Elder Neal A. Maxwell. He said, "Isn't it interesting that Jesus was the great praise giver . . . ? Much more often, we too can give others 'the garment of praise' (Isa. 61:3). There are so many people with no such clothing in their wardrobes—or only a T-shirt. They shiver for want of a little praise. Meanwhile, each of us has far more opportunities for bestowing deserved praise than we ever use!"[82]

Do you know someone who fits Elder Maxwell's description, someone who goes unnoticed and could use a little praise? Have you been waiting for just the right moment to share a compliment or some other meaningful recognition? Could you be instrumental in lifting hands that hang down and strengthening feeble knees (see D&C 81:5) with words of love and encouragement? There is no time like the present. The world is a better place and we are better people when we use our voices for good. We shouldn't underestimate our positive influence when we engage in language and conversation befitting daughters of God.

I remember a silly little game my friends and I used to play in elementary school. Play began when someone slugged someone else on the arm and whispered, "Pass it on." There were many more pleasant activities that didn't involve punching, like jumping rope, hopscotch, and four square, but for some reason this one caught on and happened more than it should have. Looking back, it's too bad we didn't pass along good things instead.

I love a little poem written by Henry Burton. These days, the phrase *pay it forward* is often used to express the same types of actions. But whether we're passing it on or paying it forward, we all want to be part of the efforts in this type of goodness that makes us better people and makes a difference in the lives of others.

> Have you had a kindness shown?
> Pass it on.
> 'Twas not given for thee alone,
> Pass it on.
> Let it travel down the years,
> Let it wipe another's tears,
> Till in heav'n the deed appears—
> Pass it on.[83]

---

82 Neal A. Maxwell, "Jesus, the Perfect Mentor," *Ensign*, Feb. 2001, 14.
83 "The Bright Side: Little Excursions into the Field of Optimism," arranged by Charles R. Skinner (New York: Frank D. Beattys & Co., 1909), 27.

By way of one terrific example, one Sunday my son Tanner was a youth speaker in sacrament meeting. After we got home from church, he tossed a small envelope onto the counter. He gave me permission to read the card tucked inside. It was a kind note from Brother Scott Pearce, a fellow ward member. He wanted to let Tanner know how much he'd enjoyed his talk. Brother Pearce also mentioned a specific principle from the talk that he was going to apply in his own life. I was so impressed by the gesture that I've kept an eye on Brother Pearce since then, and I've noticed him handing out notes to others following their speaking assignments. Pass it on indeed!

We can pay attention and say hello to those we pass in the hall at church or in our neighborhoods. We can also acknowledge our fellow ward and stake members when we see them away from Sunday worship. If we hear a lesson or a talk in sacrament meeting that touches us, we can extend a thank-you. Since we are all teachers in this Church, a kind word lets our fellow teachers know that we don't take for granted the time and effort expended in our behalf, especially since everything we do in the Church is on a volunteer basis.

Another way we can pass along what we know about the worth of souls is by reaching out to neighbors and those we don't know well but with whom we come in limited contact during the course of our days. We can be friendly. A warm hello goes a long way. Showing courtesy at the grocery store, in a parking lot, or on the road doesn't hurt either. We can actively look for the good in others and practice accentuating the positive qualities in those we meet and interact with every day.

When the scriptures speak of the worth of souls, they relate to every person who has ever lived or ever will live. We may not all share common values, goals, or beliefs, but as children of God we do share a common heritage—the nurse, the lawyer, the teacher, the stay-at-home mom, the factory worker—everyone. The scriptures remind us that "God is no respecter of persons" (Acts 10:34), and all are precious in His sight (see Jacob 2:21). We can grow our relationships with love and respect and appreciate the variety in God's wide and glorious garden. He knows that we can love, lift, and learn from each other. He also knows that in so doing, we lift ourselves as well.

Chapter Sixteen
If the Shoe Fits

An awareness of our gifts would surely help us feel a greater sense of self-worth and a greater appreciation for God's love in giving them to us, give us a clearer understanding of who we are and how we can best contribute, help us use our resources more confidently, and allow us to better develop our talents.[84] —Anya Bateman

EVEN THOUGH I LEFT MY childhood behind long ago, I am not ashamed to admit that I still love a good fairy tale almost as much as the average six-year-old. I hope you do too. Grimms' *Cinderella* happens to be one of the most recognizable stories about princesses on the planet and is one of my personal favorites. There's a lot to like about any tale that includes mice who magically turn into horses and a sparkling carriage that springs from a squash all because of a fairy godmother, who appears from nowhere just in the nick of time. In my opinion, though, the real story is in the glass slippers.

Skipping the familiar backstory, let's fast forward to the royal ball at midnight, Cindy's curfew. In all the dancing and merriment, she has not forgotten what her fairy godmother told her—the magic ends at midnight. Hence, at the last chime of the clock before twelve, Cinderella reluctantly but swiftly flees. In her haste, she leaves behind one glass slipper. As it turns out, losing the slipper is fortuitous for her since it's the only real evidence the prince has that the girl of his dreams exists. (It's also more evidence that it's all about the glass slipper, since without this turn of events the story would have come to an abrupt and disappointing end.)

After the ball, the prince cannot forget his enchanting dance partner. He and his footmen traverse the entire kingdom on a quest for her. As fate would have it, they eventually end up at Cinderella's out-of-the-way abode. Her stepmother has locked her away so her delightful stepsisters can try on the slipper uninterrupted, a last and desperate attempt to win the prince's hand.

---

84 Anya Bateman, "If Your Talents Come Incognito," *Ensign*, Jun. 1991, 62.

Alas, when the shoe is presented, no matter how hard those disagreeable girls try, it doesn't fit because that glass slipper was made especially for Cinderella.

Have you tried, like Cindy's stepsisters, to fit into someone else's shoes? And I'm not referring to walking a mile in another's footwear to get a better idea of their trials. I'm talking about trying to be something or someone we're not or wishing we were more like somebody else. It's a little like stuffing our feet into shoes that aren't the right size. It's going to get uncomfortable. The most predictable result is that we're going to end up with a few blisters, or at least very sore feet.

The pumpkin-turned-carriage in Cinderella's story reminds me of a silly cantaloupe I once knew that pretended to be something else. Years ago, my daughter Whitney decided to try her hand at gardening. With the help of a good friend, who was also a skilled gardener, she turned a patch of uncultivated ground in our backyard into a lovely spot where fruits and vegetables flourished. In one corner, she planted cantaloupe. Before long we saw the beginnings of fruit on the vine. Eventually, there was one melon that grew and ripened faster than any others. I watched it carefully until it was ready. I could almost taste it the day I picked it from the garden, with Whitney's permission, of course. My mouth watered as the first slice revealed the typical peachy-orange color that looked so refreshing and inviting. The first bite was an entirely different story. Even though everything on the inside and outside of that attractive melon said cantaloupe, it tasted exactly like a cucumber. I couldn't get it out of my mouth fast enough. Real gardeners may not have reached the same conclusion, but my less-than-expert opinion told me that the close proximity of the cantaloupe to the patch of cucumbers was the source of the trouble. The cantaloupe left me terribly disappointed, but not because it tasted like a cucumber. Cucumbers are my favorite vegetable, especially bathed in vinegar and salt. The problem arose because I expected something else. Whatever happened in the signal that my eyes and brain sent to my mouth made my poor taste buds shudder.

The lesson for us in the glass slipper and the cantaloupe masquerading as a cucumber is this—there is no need for us to be something we're not or wish we were more like somebody else. We are divinely created to be different. Each one of us can contribute in diverse and special ways. We have unique talents, abilities, and gifts from our Heavenly Father. One of the important and ongoing quests of our lives is to identify our own gifts and pray to understand how best to use them in forwarding God's work.

Some gifts or talents are less noticeable and have to be discovered. Others seem to flow without much effort. Some are visible, like singing, painting, performing, or public speaking. Others include decorating, organizing, or running a home. There are also many talents not as easily seen but every bit as valuable and worthwhile. If those are the gifts you possess, they are remarkable. Among them are service, compassion, thoughtfulness, lending a listening ear, or always knowing the right thing to say. Others are spirituality, faithfulness, or always being prepared. The list goes on and on and is as diverse as we are. In addition, as we age and grow, there is always room to add to what we already know and do well.

Our Heavenly Father has asked us to continually discover and develop our talents. Working toward our full potential helps eliminate the things that limit us by connecting with those God-given qualities. Any time we strive to improve ourselves or learn something new, we are better for it. Our confidence increases. We are more self-assured and comfortable with who we are and what we have to offer. Broader horizons open to our view, and new opportunities often present themselves. We are also more generous and accepting of others.

Creativity is in and of itself a connection to our Father in Heaven. The works of His hands are masterpieces. He designed the plan of happiness for us. He planned and arranged for the creation of this glorious world. He created each of us in His own image. According to President Dieter F. Uchtdorf:

> The desire to create is one of the deepest yearnings of the human soul. No matter our talents, education, backgrounds, or abilities, we each have an inherent wish to create something that did not exist before.
>
> . . . [R]emember that you are spirit daughters of the most creative Being in the universe.[85]

Developing our talents doesn't end because we've reached adulthood. Rather, it's a lifelong quest that enables us to keep discovering, learning, and giving. Hence, we never outgrow the opportunity to grow. We can continually find or add to the creative qualities within us that, in turn, connect us to our Father. We begin by identifying something that sparks an interest or seems challenging. Sometimes trying something new is exactly what we need. Perhaps we admire a gift or ability in someone else or we see a need we could fill. We can also pray and ask our Heavenly Father what He has in mind for us. After we identify, we create a plan to learn all we can, practice, study, and observe. There are classes to take, books to read, and myriad other resources right at our fingertips like never before. In addition, we can reach out to others for help and encouragement.

---

85 Dieter F. Uchtdorf, "Happiness, Your Heritage," *Ensign*, Nov. 2008, 118.

Keep in mind that in the process of identifying new interests and developing gifts and talents, putting too much pressure on ourselves to do something perfectly might just push us to the point of giving up. I learned that firsthand in a miserable way on a ski slope. Some of my friends were good skiers, and I thought I could be one too, even though I struggled to walk and chew bubblegum at the same time. I got skis one Christmas, and my friends and I hit the slopes for the first time a few days later. Our approach was all wrong from the outset. Did I take lessons or do any research? No. The only thing I knew was how to snowplow, sort of. I'd never done it—my friends had only told me about it, and frankly, it didn't seem that hard.

Once at the resort and emboldened by the encouragement of my pals, I strapped on my skis, skipped the bunny hills, and headed straight to the top of the mountain—no lessons, limited instruction, and not one ounce of skill. I didn't even really know how to get on and off the lift. My first run took forever— at least. (To top it all off, while I was lying on that mountainside trying to get up after each fall, I had to endure comments from a couple of cute guys I knew who made five trips to my one.) It was a disaster! When I finally reached the base of the hill, I rested briefly and half-heartedly tried again, figuring the second attempt had to be better than the first. This time I got caught in a thick fog at the top of the mountain. Since I couldn't see one ski in front of the other and was unfamiliar with the terrain, I had to follow a more experienced skier by holding on to her waist as she slowly led me to safety. It was so merciful of her to help me, but I was mortified! If it wasn't for her, I might still be there. Sadly, I failed miserably because I hadn't done my research or spent any time practicing. I thought it looked easy. I expected too much at once and have never been back.

We don't have to be perfect in our attempts when discovering and developing our talents. It's okay to give ourselves permission to acknowledge that we're not trying to be everything—only improving one day at a time. We are each a work in progress, and we can only be the best version of ourselves. In the process, there is lots of wiggle room, potential for improvement, and trying and trying again.

We should also be careful about taking on too much at once. I'm reminded of our old friend Marcia from a classic episode of *The Brady Bunch*. She is worried about fitting in as a new freshman in high school, especially since most of her good friends are attending a different school. As Mike and Carol address her concerns, they innocently mention that joining a club might get her off to a good start and help her find her place. The overachieving Marcia takes it to a different level. She decides that if one club is good, more is definitely better. She writes her name on the roster of every single club, from karate to scuba diving. Even if you've never seen the episode, you can probably guess that it is all too much, especially after Peter's volcano science project sprays faux lava all over the prestigious members of the booster organization in her school, ruining Marcia's chances of joining their elite group. At the episode's conclusion, she decides to quit all the clubs except ceramics, because it suits her best.

So, what happens if after all our hard work there is still someone who plays the flute, ties a quilt, paints a picture, or organizes their home better than we do or could ever hope to? We learn from the Savior's parable that as we make an effort to develop the talents we've been given, what we already have will be added upon (see Matt. 25:14–30).

Having been blessed with so much, none of us should have the slightest regret or feel short-changed because we haven't inherited all the talents we would like or because we see abilities in others we wish we had in more abundance ourselves. If we were all the same, how would we differentiate between what God has given to us for our role in building His kingdom on this earth and what He has given someone else? It would be like having only one choice at the ice cream store or the candy counter. It's the variety that keeps things interesting.

If you could choose any talent in the world that you don't already have, what would it be? (We're not coveting here—just identifying.) Allow me to go first. I would like to sing. Not with just an adequate carry-a-tune type of voice, but a glorious instrument that stirs people and moves mountains. If I'm being honest, that is never going to happen. I simply wasn't born with that kind of gift. However, if I put forth enough effort to learn music and technique, I can certainly be a better singer than I am today. I can also appreciate and admire someone who moves people and mountains with song and recognize that I might be able to accomplish the same thing in a completely different way.

When we understand the gospel of Jesus Christ, the talents and accomplishments of others do not diminish us, even when we see those who seem to have them all. All our talents glorify our Maker. With an eye single to Him, we can admire talents in others and celebrate individual successes without comparing. It's like the old adage that warns against seeing the apple the same way we do an orange. Both are delicious in different ways, but to compare them against each other to determine which is best would be unfair since they are two very different types of fruit. As we understand who we are, we realize we are created equal but we're not all the same, by divine design. Often, we find that the more we get to know and love each other, the more we have in common in deeper, more meaningful ways.

We've already spoken of Cinderella and her glass slippers. I have a couple of shoe stories of my own. They don't involve a fairy godmother and they're not nearly as magical, but they do illustrate a supporting point. One involves a shopping trip with my daughter Chelsey, who was looking for dress shoes to complement a cute skirt she had already purchased. We'd nearly exhausted our options as we stepped into the last shoe store in the mall. There were boxes and boxes of shoes stacked from front to back and side to side. We were in a hurry, so she went one way and I went the other. Since I was buying, I showed her some sensible shoes that would go with everything. She showed me everything else. She tried on many shoes and finally settled on some turquoise high heels with a faux snakeskin finish. I had to agree they were perfect for her and just right for her new skirt!

I have forever been practical black pumps, even when I was young. She is darling, daring aqua heels, and she always has been. She doesn't love me any less or hold it against me because I'm careful and not particularly in touch with current trends. I love her for her fashion flair and her enthusiasm that shows in the way she dresses and how she lives her life. We are different, but it doesn't change the way we feel about each other.

I learned something from another pair of shoes one crystal-clear spring morning when my husband and I attended a wedding in the Manti Utah Temple. We passed the recommend desk, descended a flight of stairs, and moved on to the marriage waiting room. Like everyone else, we left our shoes on one of the available racks.

Unhurried, I took the opportunity to peruse the variety of shoes that lined the racks outside the waiting room. My black pumps joined others with high heels, low heels, and no heels. There were men's loafers and polished dress shoes and women's shoes of varied styles and sizes. Since most of the shoes were black or brown, a pair of bright-pink sandals stood out to me. Intrigued, I wondered who might belong to them. Was she single, married, blonde, brunette, young, old, or somewhere in between? I looked around the room. I couldn't tell. I would have loved to identify her to satisfy my curiosity, but unless I stalked the shoe racks to wait for her return, I was never going to know. (I was not above doing that, but I had a marriage to attend.)

Even though I never found out who wore those peppy pink sandals to the temple that day, the message was clear. Each pair of shoes represented individuals from different walks of life with varied roles, responsibilities, professions, and talents. One of the significant lessons of the temple is that as we leave those worldly identifiers behind, we are better able to see each other in a different light. Whether we wear pink shoes, black shoes, green shoes, or no shoes, we all have talents, abilities, and characteristics that allow us to contribute in our own way. God sees all of us the same way and loves us each for who we are.

All our talents, however many or few, are needed to build each other and to participate in God's great work on this earth. We shouldn't let the talents and successes of our brothers and sisters get in the way or undermine how we feel about ourselves. Nor should our talents and differences divide us or detract from our interactions and relationships.

There are numerous good gifts to develop and practically unlimited creative opportunities to pursue throughout our lives. It is a wise steward who identifies and develops those gift and qualities and uses them to serve God. When we create, our worth is not based on results. It is based on who we already are, full of eternal promise. God knows our hearts and what we have the potential to become. The Giver of all good gifts (see James 1:17) celebrates our talents and our individuality. Why shouldn't we?

Chapter Seventeen
Happy Endings

You are elect. You are of noble birth. Don't compromise your divine inheritance. You were born to be a queen.[86] —Elaine S. Dalton

WHEN WE TALK ABOUT ROYALTY, we're most likely to think of princes and princesses, kings and queens, castles and happily-ever-afters. In an earlier chapter, I confessed that in younger years I often imagined my world would be filled with one magical moment after another. Initially, I was surprised when the story of my life didn't always meet those expectations. Maybe you've had occasion to feel the same way. However, after a lot of contemplation and experience, I've come to know that even though our days may not consist of stately halls and fancy balls, and we probably won't bask in the luxuries afforded earthly royalty, there *is* wonder in recognizing the endless nature of our worth and our lives. There is majesty in our eternal heritage. There is joy in our days, magic in moments, enchantment in the beautiful world around us, and experiences that take our breath away. We find fascination and fulfillment in precious time spent with family and friends, hope and happiness in living the gospel of Jesus Christ, and sweet assurance in the promise of eternity.

Our Heavenly Father sent us to earth to gain experience and prepare us to be with Him again forever. But it's not just about trudging through and holding on. He wants us to be happy on the way. Much of the joy we find in life is connected in a real way to how we feel about ourselves. There is much good for us to do and enjoy here before we get there. Elder Jeffrey R. Holland shared this remarkable thought: "God is eagerly waiting for the chance to answer your prayers and fulfill your dreams, just as He always has. But He can't if you don't pray, and He can't if you don't dream. In short, He can't if you don't believe."[87]

86 Elaine S. Dalton, "Remember Who You Are!" *Ensign*, May 2010, 122.
87 Jeffrey R. Holland, "This, the Greatest of All Dispensations," *Ensign*, Jul. 2007, 54.

Believe is a wonderful, powerful word that encompasses faith, hope, and trust. There are many things we can believe in the world today, but placing our belief in things that matter will make the most difference for us here. It's important to believe in ourselves, in what we can do and who we are as beloved daughters of Heavenly Father. The core of our belief and the basis for our faith is that Jesus Christ is the Only Begotten of the Father, the Savior of the world, the key to our progression, and the promise of things to come. We believe in His teachings. We have faith in His word. In the gospel of Jesus Christ, it is belief that keeps us grounded yet gives us wings. A lot of magic happens when someone believes.

I loved the story of Peter Pan when I was young, mostly because I share a name with one of the main characters. A favorite scene happens early in the Disney movie when Peter tries to teach Wendy and her brothers to fly. The Darling siblings can't seem to get their feet off the ground with happy thoughts alone. They are only able to take flight with three additional elements—faith, trust, and pixie dust. Pixie dust might be in short supply in your home, as it is in mine, but in my book, hope serves as an excellent substitute. Additionally, in real life, miracles happen and mountains are moved because of faith and trust.

Many years ago, I was part of a group that organized and implemented a stake youth conference that was not the typical experience our young people were accustomed to. Because of the way it was designed, and due to the goals we'd set, we couldn't release much information. The conference commenced late one summer evening as we divided the young men and women into groups mostly made up of youth from other wards they didn't know well or at all. After a short meeting at the church, we drove out into the darkness toward the designated camping area. Upon arrival at the base of our destination, we set out on a trail, flashlights in hand, for a faith hike up the mountain to a place that hadn't been disclosed. You might guess that some of the youth were worried. You would be right! We were with them the whole way, but since we couldn't answer every question or alleviate all their concerns, our response was simply, "Trust us." Miraculously and to their great credit, they did. It wasn't an easy process, as worthwhile things seldom are. Some of the conference activities stretched youth and leaders alike in ways we didn't think possible, but we ended up having an incredible spiritual experience that left a lasting impression. And it all began because of trust.

Trust in the Lord is a significant part of the equation in mortality. It is trust, coupled with the faith and belief we have in our Heavenly Father and Jesus Christ, that moves us forward and keeps us reaching and striving even when we don't understand the reason for everything right now. As we believe the gospel of Jesus Christ, hope in what's to come, and trust in our Savior's redeeming love, we find meaning and direction in the choices we make here. May we ever be able to say, as Nephi once exulted, "O Lord, I have trusted in thee, and I will trust in thee forever" (2 Ne. 4:34).

Our Father in Heaven and Savior are worthy of our trust. As perfect beings, they will not let us down or forsake us. We are daughters of God, joint heirs with Jesus Christ, whose name we took upon ourselves at baptism. Because of what we know about our royal lineage and heritage, it is our great privilege to honor Them by doing all we can to live by Their teachings. Because of what we know, we must conduct ourselves in a way befitting that heritage. To paraphrase something President Harold B. Lee once said, we must "be loyal to the royal within [us]."[88] That loyalty will be rewarded in this life and most especially in the life to come.

What will things be like for us in the eternal kingdom of our Father? The question takes me back to the days when my dear father planned our almost-annual summer family vacations, which were the highlight of my young life. He loved to travel and spared no effort to meticulously schedule our itinerary almost down to the minute. Because the Internet had yet to be invented, he sent away for pamphlets from the travel bureaus of the cities and towns of our anticipated destinations. The brochures he got back were filled with glossy photos and lively descriptions of the things to see and do along our route. I can still picture him thumbing through the literature he received, map in hand, as he plotted the journey and highlighted waypoints that would make up our vacation each year.

Since we traveled not by plane but in the family station wagon, everywhere we went, there were plenty of opportunities and needed breaks from the road, especially with our active crew crammed into a tight space. It was all those stops along the way that made our experiences amazing! I remember strolling through the lovely Butchart Gardens in beautiful Victoria, Canada, looking up at the giant sequoias of California, shivering inside the ice caves of Shoshone, Idaho, and experiencing numerous breathtaking spots in-between. Though we didn't usually travel very far, Dad and Mom gave us as much of the world as they could.

Loving parent that He is, our Father in Heaven wants to give us everything He has. I am not well-traveled, and I've never had a passport, but I don't have to go very far to know that however grand our earthly destinations may be, they cannot compare to the destiny that awaits us in His heavenly kingdom.

88 See Harold B. Lee, "Be Loyal to the Royal Within You" (Brigham Young University devotional, Sept. 11, 1973); speeches.byu.edu.

That destiny is not only a place; it encompasses all we hope to become as well. The reward our Father has in store for us should tell us something about how He feels about each one of us.

There are no glossy pamphlets or fancy brochures of what life in the life after this will be. I looked. There are a few clues in the scriptures. We read in Corinthians, "Eye has not seen, nor ear heard, neither have entered into the heart of man, the things which God hath prepared for them that love him" (1 Cor. 2:9). We know there are kingdoms, but we don't have a physical description of the wonder and beauty and peace in that place, nor could we possibly grasp the splendor of it all with our finite minds. The Savior spoke of mansions when He addressed His Apostles at the Last Supper. He said, "In my Father's house are many mansions: if it were not so, I would have told you. I go to prepare a place for you" (John 14:2).

In mortality, we measure mansions in square footage. I don't know how big a home has to be to qualify, but in earthly terms they are generally large elegant estates with lots of rooms, surrounded by acreage, manicured gardens, and maybe even a swimming pool or two. Success in our world is often measured by the square footage of wealth, position, or accumulations. God's mansions are not measured that way but in glory, intelligences, and eternal lives. Additionally, we've been reminded that God doesn't use any of the world's measurements to gauge us. He uses our hearts.

Hearkening back to the tale of Cinderella at the royal ball, the magic may have ended for her at midnight, but we know there is no end to our eternal joy and reward. Just like some of the elements of these enchanted tales from childhood, in between the very good in our lives, there are sometimes thorns that hedge up our way, dragons to be conquered, and villains who hope to thwart our progress by distracting us from our true potential and by trying to convince us we aren't who we know we are. The true story for us is that our Heavenly Father has promised us happy endings if we trust and follow Him. That's why it's vitally important for us to never lose sight of who we are and to never forget His love and our potential.

President Boyd K. Packer once compared our lives to a three-act play. He explained, "'And they all lived happily ever after' is never written into the second act. That line belongs in the third act when the mysteries are solved and everything is put right."[89]

Happy endings are not for fairy tales alone. In the story of our lives, along with thrilling tales of success and adventure, however bad it gets, no

89 Boyd K. Packer, "The Play and the Plan" (CES fireside, May 7, 1995), accessed December 11, 2017, http://emp.byui.edu/huffr/The%20Play%20and%20the%20Plan%20--%20 Boyd%20K.%20Packer.htm.

matter the struggle, because of all that our loving Father and Savior have done, there is the glorious possibility of a happy ending on the final page. We don't know all that life will bring to us, but the end is known. Good will triumph, righteousness will eventually prevail, and our Father will bring us home. What matters most is what side of the battle we're on.

Our Heavenly Father sees us as we are, loves us because we are His, and knows more than anyone else what we can become. One of the most important things we can do in this life is to remember our divine heritage and to live every day in a way becoming to daughters of the King of Heaven. He has blessed us with the promise and potential to become queens. As we make our way back to Him, we must never forget that the story we write here takes a lifetime—our lifetime. Just like any other compelling story, there will be lots of twists and turns in the plot. But even if all the endings aren't perfect here, when we stay on the path and keep our destination in sight, our story continues, and our happy ending awaits us in the eternal kingdom of our Father.

About the Author

In addition to watching *Murder She Wrote* reruns, sewing, writing, and creating, Wendy Ellison works at her favorite and most important roles of daughter, wife, mother, and grandmother. She understands firsthand the challenges Latter-day Saint women face as they juggle their many responsibilities and face the growing difficulties of our day. Wendy believes the best chance for success and happiness in this life is found in living the principles of the gospel of Jesus Christ. Through trying and trying again, she is striving every day to let the feelings she has about herself match her worth as a daughter of God and would love for all women to measure themselves the same way. Wendy is anxious to add her voice of encouragement to the efforts of sisters everywhere to be happy, faithful, powerful women, filled with confidence, fortified by truth, and fully prepared to realize their infinite potential.